If it wasn't for the money, I wouldn't be doing this

If it wasn't for the money, I wouldn't be doing this

Finding the courage to survive a job you hate

Jenni Lans

HarperBusiness
An imprint of HarperCollins*Publishers*

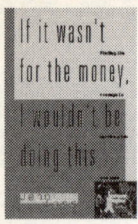

HarperBusiness
An imprint of HarperCollins*Publishers*

First published in Australia in 1996
by HarperCollins*Publishers* Pty Limited
ACN 009 913 517
A member of the HarperCollins*Publishers* (Australia) Pty Limited Group

Copyright © Jenni Lans 1996

Certain events and situations described in this book are based on actual experiences, but names have been changed.

This book is copyright.
Apart from any fair dealing for the purposes of private study, research, criticism or review, as permitted under the Copyright Act, no part may be reproduced by any process without written permission.
Inquiries should be addressed to the publishers.

HarperCollins*Publishers*
25 Ryde Road, Pymble, Sydney, NSW 2073, Australia
31 View Road, Glenfield, Auckland 10, New Zealand
77–85 Fulham Palace Road, London W6 8JB, United Kingdom
Hazelton Lanes, 55 Avenue Road, Suite 2900, Toronto, Ontario M5R 3L2
and 1995 Markham Road, Scarborough, Ontario M1B 5M8, Canada
10 East 53rd Street, New York NY 10032, USA

National Library of Australia Cataloguing-in-Publication data:

Lans, Jenni.
  If it wasn't for the money I wouldn't be doing this:
  finding the courage to survive a job you hate.

  Bibliography.
  ISBN 0 7322 5679 8.

  1. Success. 2. Job satisfaction. 3. Personality and
  occupation. 4. Prediction of occupational success.
  I. Title.

658.31422

Cover and internal design: Melanie Feddersen
Printed in Australia by Griffin Paperbacks, Adelaide on 79 gsm Bulky Paperback

9 8 7 6 5 4 3 2 1
99 98 97 96

To my inspiring and
original sister,
Rebecca Jane Lans,
who propped open
her eyelids with
matchsticks to read
copy and laughed at
all my jokes.
The limited-edition
commemorative
medal (plus bonus
gilt-edged certificate)
is on its way
to you . . .

Contents

About the author	xiv
Acknowledgments	xv

~~one~~ Are you working in a job you hate?   1

THE DOMINO EFFECT	1
IS IT SALVAGEABLE?	3
THE WORK SCALE OF HORROR	4
True Crimes — Real Life Story 1	6

~~two~~ The real rules of getting ahead   9

THE IMPERSONATION	10
PLAYING IN THE SANDPIT	11
POWER IS EVERYTHING	12
BURNING ZEPPELINS	13

~~three~~ How to survive a job you hate   15

THE POISONED CHALICE	15
IMPROVING YOUR ATTITUDE	16
THE HALF-FULL/HALF-EMPTY SYNDROME	16
DAYDREAMING	17
MENTAL HEALTH DAYS	18
LIFE RAFT	18

AFTERNOON COFFEE	19
PLOTTING AND SCHEMING	19
AM I PARANOID?	19
THE RULES OF SUCCESS	20
True Crimes — Real Life Story 2	22

~~four~~ New kid on the block — the basics   25

CORPORATE STRUCTURE	26
Chain-of-command	28
Direct report — keeping Dick or Jane happy	28
Job description	29
Federal and state industrial awards	30
Union action	32
Government policy	33
Sexual harassment	33
True Crimes — Real Life Story 3	35
Discrimination	40
PLAYING HAPPY FAMILIES — THE CORPORATE CULTURE	41
The laid-back company	41
The snap and scrabble company	42
The bottom line company	43
The el cheapo company	43
The public sector	44
WHO'S WHO	45
THE 9 TO 5 MYTH	46
SUSSING OUT OTHER PEOPLE'S AGENDAS	46
True Crimes — Real Life Story 4	47
True Crimes — Real Life Story 5	48
TRUST	51
MANNERS	52
WHERE TO STAND WHEN THE SHIT IS HITTING THE FAN	53

~~five~~ Identifying alien types 55

THE MEN FROM MARS	55
The New Age Sage	55
Mr Credibility	56
The Postwar Depressionist	57
The Great Pretender	58
The Good Bloke	59
The Empire Builder	60
THE WOMEN FROM VENUS	61
The Control Freak	61
The Boss's Wife	62
Daddy's Little Girl	63
The Obstacle Maker	64
The Corporate Girlie	65
The Two-Faced Bitch	66

~~six~~ Things you should know about work that nobody ever told you 69

PERCEPTION IS REALITY	69
AVOIDING BECOMING THE PHANTOM — BEING VISIBLE	70
True Crimes — Real Life Story 6	70
IDENTIFYING CORPORATE MYTHS	71
Work is a democracy	71
THE BROWNIE POINTS ACCUMULATOR	72
They're running the place, they must be intelligent	74
They're in menial positions, they must be dumb	75
It's not personal	75
UNDERSTANDING THE PETER PRINCIPLE	75
SEX AND GOSSIP	76

WORK FUNCTIONS AND SOCIAL FUNCTIONS	76
AVOIDING THE TAG OF VILLAGE IDIOT —	
WHAT TO SAY WHEN YOU'RE STUCK IN THE LIFT WITH THE MD	76
THE WINDOW OF OPPORTUNITY	77
THE CLAYTON'S DEADLINE	77
WHEN TO TELL A LITTLE WHITE LIE	77
GETTING THROUGH YAWNO MEETINGS	78
The agenda	78
The discussion	79
Other matters	80
Minutes	81
TRANSLATING THE LANGUAGE — AN INTRODUCTION TO WORKSPEAK	82
ASKING QUESTIONS	84
ANSWERING QUESTIONS	86
HOW TO USE MEMOS	87
The information memo	88
The protection memo	88
The warning memo	90
VISIONS, VALUES AND OTHER CORPORATE FAIRYTALES —	
SURVIVING CORPORATE TRAINING TECHNIQUES	92
The grand vision	92
The induction process	93
The psychological test	93
Team building, management and other in-house programs	94
WHO IS MY AUDIENCE?	95
MAKE ALLIES NOT ENEMIES	95
True Crimes — Real Life Story 7	97

~~seven~~ Looking, talking and acting smart   99

WOMEN	101
The suit	101
The blouse	102

Accessories	102
Make-up	103
Fashion no-nos	103
MEN	104
The suit	105
Shirts	105
Ties	107
Shoes, socks and belts	108
Jewellery and accessories	109
Fashion no-nos	109
GROOMING	110
True Crimes — Real Life Story 8	111
ATTITUDE	112
Body talk	113
What are they really thinking?	114
ETIQUETTE	114
The telephone	115
The knock	115
Looking through papers	115
The paper chase	116
Terms of endearment — addressing others	117
The introduction	118
True Crimes — Real Life Story 9	119
Small talk	120
THE PLOTTING AND SCHEMING CHECKLIST	122

~~eight~~ What to do when things go horribly wrong 125

UGLY SCENES	125
DEFENSIVE TECHNIQUES	126
Character assassination	126
Lying	127
Threatening	127

The confession	128
Pointing the finger	129
Pretending to be really, really nice	129
Ruling through fear — the bend-over technique	130
Number crunching	131
Planting mines	131
True Crimes — Real Life Story 10	132
Going for the jugular — the set-up	134
Avoiding the ambush	134
The diary	134
Human nature — letting the boss know they're the boss	135
True Crimes — Real Life Story 11	138
GOING OVER THEIR HEADS	140
The warning memo	142
The meeting	142
The second warning memo	143
The third warning memo	144
Taking legal action	144
True Crimes — Real Life Story 12	145
GET YOUR MONKEY OFF MY BACK	147
True Crimes — Real Life Story 13	148
DELEGATION — PASSING ON THE DOOMED PET PROJECT	150
AVOIDING THE BOOMERANG EFFECT	151
PHRASES THAT WILL GET YOU OUT OF TROUBLE — MORE WORKSPEAK	152
QUESTIONS YOU SHOULD NEVER ANSWER HONESTLY	154
QUESTIONS YOU SHOULD ALWAYS ANSWER HONESTLY	154
FOOT-IN-MOUTH DISEASE	155

~~nino~~ Resignation, dismissal or retrenchment   157

RECOGNISING THE DANGER SIGNALS OF AN IMMINENT SACKING	157
True Crimes — Real Life Story 14	158

RESIGNATION LETTERS	160
THE BRONZE HANDSHAKE: RETRENCHMENT AND REDUNDANCY	163
MAKING THE MOST OF YOUR EXIT INTERVIEW	164
GETTING RID OF INCRIMINATING EVIDENCE	165
REFERENCES	166

~~ten~~ Getting over it and getting on with it — 167

WORK IS NOT YOUR LIFE	167
WHAT THE HELL AM I DOING HERE?	168
PHILOSOPHY, MORALS AND ETHICS	169
True Crimes — Real Life Story 15	170
THE BIG PICTURE — RETAINING PERSPECTIVE	171
RUNNING AWAY MONEY	171
WHY CAN'T YOU LAUGH ABOUT IT?	172
True Crimes — Real Life Story 16	172
TAKING RESPONSIBILITY	173
COMMON SENSE	174
RESPECT	174
True Crimes — Real Life Story 17	175
INSTINCT	176
THE LAST WORD	177
People who can help you	179
Glossary of terms	181
Useful books to read	183
Useful films to see	185

About the author

Jenni Lans was born in Adelaide but moved to Sydney in 1985, after completing her degree, to achieve her ambition of owning a number of tailored Italian suits and a very fast white car in which to display them. During her career (in the financial sector, a brief stint running a late night coffee shop, in the film industry and the arts) she has encountered any number of vicious corporate beasties, and has been left with knuckles that drag along the ground from carrying files home on the bus. This book is the result of her experiences in the corporate jungle which she hopes will keep people grudge-free with their faith in human nature intact. She now lives quietly at home and, when not caring for her pet hampster and making macramé baskets, is a marketing consultant and freelance writer.

Acknowledgments

The following idealists and philosophers, masquerading as cynical, jaded, bitter, hostile and petty people, were most helpful in writing this book: Leonard and Patricia Lans for their irreverent view of life and their perpetual cry of 'Sit down! Tell us about your life!', Wayne Bailey ('I know the Mother Ship is coming to get me soon, what's taking it so long?'), Naomi Bailey, the only, the ultimate John Gallagher, Jane Willcox, John ('some people are comets and some people are stars') Lans, Phillip Kelly, Alec Chalmers, Mark Davis, Rachel Lans, Frank Fontanelli, Antonella Gambotto, George Marton, Carmel Boyle, Michael Karagianis, Helen Karatzas (my first and most pragmatic boss), Nick X, Bill and Heidi Godwin, Bruce Harris, Rocco Fazzari, Chuck Iossi (the greatest corporate boss that ever was), Zoe Harvey, Jim O'Kane, GH, the beautiful Robert Deakin, Jonathon Hainsworth, James Williamson, Wendy Lacoon, Nicola Evans, Alex Sava, Anne Bousfield, Chris Botting, Eddie Clunies-Ross (ornament), Roslyn Mayled, Michael Armiger, Arturo Larizza, Pauline, and HarperCollins*Publishers'* truly wonderful Helen Littleton for her faith, patience and encouragement.

Are you working in a job you hate?

'I'm bored. I'm Chairman of the Bored. I'm sick. I'm sick of all my tricks. I'm sick.' IGGY POP

one

You're lying on the couch. People are speaking to you, but you don't hear them. Dirty dishes and empty Kentucky Fried Chicken containers pile up around you. During the week, the only thing that keeps you functioning is the taped episode of your favourite television program. Forgetting to tape this results in an apoplectic fit of gargantuan proportions.

At the end of the day, it's all you can do to lurch to your room, fight your way through the piles of dirty clothes, and topple into bed. When you get up in the morning, it's a choice between wearing your pyjamas or choosing the item with the appearance of having been trampled upon least.

You hate everybody, and, worse, everybody hates you.

You are in a living nightmare.

You are working in a job you hate.

THE DOMINO EFFECT

People spend over a third of their life working. When something goes wrong in one section of your life, chances are that it will start leaking into other parts of your life.

You may not realise that you're miserable, and you may not realise the cause, but here's a few telltale signs to look for:

- Upon waking, there is a sinking feeling in the pit of your stomach, a feeling not unlike heartburn, or nausea. Your head aches.
- These feelings lead you to believe that you are suffering either a heart attack, a brain tumour, or the beginning of the flu. These symptoms are not a source of concern in themselves, rather you embrace them, as your first, joyful thought is 'I may not have to go to work today'.
  The thought of contracting some horrible disease makes you think with yearning of a nice, clean hospital bed and the doing of nothing for around six weeks or so.
- Your sense of humour has sunk to an all-time low, resulting in a kind of morbid gallows humour, amusing to nobody but yourself.
- There is only one topic of conversation: work. Again, it is interesting to nobody but yourself. At first, people listen politely, but then they either zone out or walk away.
- Invitations out decrease at the same rate as your sense of humour.
- If you do happen to get an invitation out you shoot questions at the hapless inviter like a person wielding a machine-gun. 'Who's going to be there?' you snap. 'Do I have to talk to anybody?' 'All right, I'll go, but only if I don't have to talk to anybody,' in a very ungracious tone of voice. This attitude prevails at work where you find you develop an unexpected love of your office, your memos and your fax machine. Anything is better than actually having to *talk* to people.
- You fantasise about your boss being killed in a freak accident.

- You fantasise about bomb scares in your building. You place an alarm clock in a shoe box and wrap it in brown paper. You think it is convincing and think seriously about planting it in the stairwell.
- When you do finally get home from work you open the front door, head straight for the bedroom and get into bed, fully clothed, troubling only to kick off your shoes. You eat your dinner in there, which kind flatmates bring to you on a tray.
- You are the ringer of the Bell of Doom, crushing any enthusiasm, ideas or positivism with jaded and cynical responses along the lines of a sneering 'Yeah, sure', or 'Well, that won't last long'.
- The phrase 'Bring out your dead' begins to manifest an anarchic rhythm, in which you can see a certain appeal. You consider buying a bell with a doleful ring.

If you recognise any of these symptoms, you are in a bad way. There's no doubt about it: you are working in a job you hate.

DON'T PANIC!

Not every situation is impossible. What you need to do is stop the rot at its source. Letting everything slide into the mire of depression and self-indulgence is going to make it worse: you must take some control.

IS IT SALVAGEABLE?

The first thing you need to do is to determine exactly where you sit on the work Scale of Horror. You're all at sea, rolling around in billows of suspicion, paranoia and dipping confidence. You need to establish if you are on the *Titanic* or the *Queen Mary*. If you are definitely on the former, all you need to do is establish which lifeboat you're going to get into. But if you are on the latter and think, bar a few squalls occasionally, that you could manage a pleasant cruise, then chances are that the situation is salvageable. Forget the life rafts, fellas, I'm staying on board!

Examine the list of common work complaints below, and tick the ones you believe most apply to you.

THE WORK SCALE OF HORROR

- Why is everybody on the train looking at me?
- I feel ill all the time at the thought of going to work.
- My boss has given me a second warning memo.
- I have been given the 'attitude' speech.
- I am trapped in the Cone of Silence — nobody is talking to me.
- My boss is being extremely, suspiciously nice to me after lots of disagreements.
- I can't be bothered looking for another job — I'm too depressed.
- I fantasise constantly about resigning.
- I can't remember the last time I had lunch with anybody at work.
- I am not informed of meetings at all anymore. Am I invisible?
- I talk about nothing but work.
- I have been to see my union for advice.
- I have lost my sense of humour.
- I am hauled into the MD's office almost every week.
- I am afraid to go on holidays.
- The MD looks at me and appears to have difficulty recognising me.
- People attack me constantly in meetings.
- I have been to several job interviews.
- I no longer get introduced to overseas visitors.
- My boss has given me a first warning memo.
- Some people are still talking to me.

- I have been involved in only a couple of disagreements with the MD.
- I can still laugh about some things at work, but not all of them.
- I used to be asked my opinion in meetings, but not recently.
- Why is that person on the train looking at me?
- I am still having lunch with people.
- I am invited to meetings — just before they happen.
- I have received no warning memos, but a serious 'chat'.
- I look through the employment section every week, but I haven't applied for anything yet.
- The MD still says 'good morning' to me.
- I still go to meetings, am advised of them beforehand, but there are some that I feel I should be invited to but I'm not.

If your ticks proliferate around the top section of the page, then you may well be on the *Titanic*. But it is important that you examine your situation carefully before accepting that conclusion.

If your ticks are thickly arranged around the middle of the chart, then there is a possibility that the situation is worth saving. If this is the case then the cause could be a number of factors of which ignorance of how work environments operate may be the major one.

If most of your ticks are at the bottom of the chart, then you may have just started your first job or a new job, and you may not have yet come to grips with the particular circumstances of your workplace.

Having roughly decided into which category you fall, you can now read on and contemplate those issues that most apply to you.

True Crimes — Real Life Story

Carolyn's first job was as a publications officer in a large accounting firm. Being young, naive and unaware of the real rules of success in the working world, she believed that people would treat her with respect, honesty and fairness. She did the best she could: worked hard at all her projects, covered all the corners, worked late hours and was enthusiastic and polite all of the time.

'It was a very demanding job, managing all the publications for this international company. Looking back now, I'm amazed at my own naiveté, but I really thought that all you had to do was do the job and that you would be rewarded for your efforts.'

Carolyn, being somewhat shy, did not get to know the people she worked with very well, and often had trouble working out exactly what people wanted from her.

'I knew nothing,' she says. 'Absolutely nothing. I didn't know that the key to a lot of success is to fit in: that most companies would rather have somebody who does the job competently rather than brilliantly as long as they get along with everybody they work with. If people can work with you easily (and you make it look easy) there are usually no problems.'

Carolyn rarely went to work functions to get to know her work colleagues and she was deathly afraid of her boss. She made several mistakes: by not talking to enough people she remained ignorant of what the real issues of importance were (the same issues that were important to her boss); she had no idea who was currently in management's favour and therefore should be cultivated; she didn't ask enough clarifying questions to maintain her position; and she had no idea in which direction her boss was moving.

When it came, her sacking was like a bolt from the blue even though it followed a series of signs which could have helped Carolyn turn the situation around, if she had recognised them as such.

'I just didn't have a high enough profile,' says Carolyn. 'I felt uneasy and the mere presence of my boss was enough to make me make more mistakes than usual. I just felt sick. I knew I was doing something wrong, but I wasn't sure enough of myself to approach people to ask them about it. When my boss called me into his office and upbraided me, I had no idea that I was being given a "verbal warning". I just thought he was having a go at me. Following this, because I didn't handle it properly, my confidence dipped and I started stuffing up on projects that I could have done with my eyes closed before.'

Carolyn was then given a performance review which was well under par, followed up by a written memo explaining all the things she had to improve. She was also put on a weekly reporting basis with the person immediately senior to her.

'I didn't realise they were trying to shove me out,' she says. 'I didn't know that they were following all the procedures to get rid of me. I didn't know what was going on. I was sleeping nearly 16 hours a day and still feeling tired and I had lost my appetite. Of course, by the time the end came, I had become nearly as incompetent as they had intimated I was.'

The sacking was done as a form of ambush: one Friday afternoon at five o'clock, her boss came into her office, handed her a cheque and said 'Thank you very much for your time here, I hope you do well in your future career'.

'I was shocked. I can't believe I didn't see it coming. I left, in tears. Now of course I know what all the rules are, and I would never do the same thing again. The time for action was during that "verbal chat" with my boss. That's when I should have realised things were not well. I know better now.'

The real rules of getting ahead

two

'It was, I soon apprehended, a sort of kindergarten for the terminally incompetent.' BARRY HUMPHRIES, MORE PLEASE, ABOUT HIS SECOND JOB

Most problems people have at work are caused by the fact that they expect it to be just like every other aspect of their lives. We live in a democratic society and we believe, therefore, that trust, fairness and justice operate at work just as they do everywhere else. The problem is, in the work environment, they don't. Nobody knows why this is exactly, but if you mix power, kudos and money with a whole pile of human beings, whose outstanding characteristics are eccentricity and unpredictability, and add a quirky twist of new technology, the result is an environment that has *got* to be governed by some pretty weird rules.

At the moment you're in a tight spot. You either hate your job and are on the verge of losing it, or you are wandering around in a dazed manner muttering: 'Is it me? Am I going insane? Am I the only one who thinks this way?' Rest assured, you are not alone. Everybody, unless they are complete fools, thinks the same way you do, it's just that nobody ever says so. You either haven't been playing by the rules or nobody has told you what they are. You've got to work out what they are and then turn them to your advantage so that you can get some power to actually do the job you were employed to do, while having some fun along the way.

The major thing that impacts on any job are the people you work with. Remember the old saying 'You can't choose your relatives'? In exactly the same way, you can't choose the people you work with and therefore you have to put up with them. Even the most hopeless of relatives can sometimes be pulled into line by appealing to family loyalty, but you can't even rely on this with the people you work with. You know nothing about them and so it is foolish to assume that they are going to behave in any sort of reasonable manner. Why would they? You have no ties of blood or friendship, no basis of trust or loyalty from which you can assume that they *will* behave properly. (See the section 'Identifying alien types'.)

Unfortunately for everybody concerned, you have to learn a whole new set of rules that are in no way applicable to the way you normally conduct your life. It's all about blending in, chameleon-like. It's about knowing the right way to dress, to act and to speak. It's about knowing the difference between the corporate *structure* and the corporate *culture*, not to mention the unwritten rules. Break even one of these rules and it's like a snow-covered rock falling down a hill. It may stop, but break another rule and before you know it, it's careering down the slope, becoming bigger and bigger until it becomes an avalanche. We know it's not fair, we know it's not just, but this is the way it really is and you're going to have to learn to play the game to get ahead.

THE IMPERSONATION

The lunatic fringe believes that aliens are walking among us in human guise and that underneath the convincing *Homo sapiens* mask is quite a different creature. (A lot of people would say they know who they are: born-again Christians.)

Just as aliens adopt a whole new persona to walk among us without causing undue alarm, you too must create a stage character and give a very good impersonation of a person who actually likes working.

You do this in one very simple way: *becoming* the part. You've got to camouflage yourself, your real personality and intentions, by blending into the background and looking, acting and talking just like everybody else, as you will see in the section on 'Looking, talking and acting smart'. They must never, ever see the true person behind the mask. Most people are extremely judgmental, whether they mean to be or not, and the bit of your personality that may peek out accidentally may be the one thing that everybody else highly disapproves of.

By the time you have finished your career, you will believe that you should be the one collecting the Academy Award for *Forrest Gump*. After all, that wasn't such an amazing performance. All Hanks did was pretend to be retarded, whereas you are pretending to be somebody else entirely, somebody fair, just and very, very nice, which is a far greater ask.

PLAYING IN THE SANDPIT

You will need to remind yourself constantly at work that you are not, strictly speaking, dealing with adults. You are dealing with childish beings who react in essentially selfish and unfair ways, but who have the effrontery to cover it all over with a veneer of sophistication.

Imagine a giant sandpit. There you all are, playing with your toys, absorbed and happy in your own little world. Suddenly, a large child appears, and roughly kicking sand in your face, takes away that electric tractor that Father Christmas gave you. You're left sitting there, tears cascading through the sand on your face. You want your tractor back. It belongs to you. Not only does this unscrupulous person have your toy, he has all the others too and seems to show no desire to share any of them.

Who is this person? Quite obviously, his character is of a very low nature.

Briefly, you look at the other children. An insurrection? Perhaps, if you all joined together you could stick his head in the sand and overwhelm him, getting back what is rightly yours. But Billy is crying weakly already: he has no desire to lose one of only four new teeth he has. There is already a spectacular gap when he smiles. Andrea is afraid of mucking up her dress: her mother sends her to her room when this happens. As for Sam, he's humming while he makes a sandcastle. He's forgotten all about it.

This is when you realise that you can't rely on these spineless creatures for anything at all. Revolution? Forget it! They're too concerned about themselves. They are quite willing to forgo a toy for a while in order to avoid being involved in any ugly scenes. *You* have to get your toy back *yourself* and you're going to have to think up some pretty devious schemes to get it.

POWER IS EVERYTHING

The only way to achieve anything meaningful is to get some power. Since you spend a large amount of time at work, it would be a good thing if you could enjoy yourself and do a few things while you're there. You won't ever be able to do anything of note when someone else is telling you what to do. By learning defensive techniques like avoiding the ambush and the boomerang, lying, threatening, cheating and the infamous bend-over manoeuvre, you will be able to grab a bit of power for yourself and have a good time while you're doing it. The way to get power is to get as much information as you can about everybody and everything. Keep this in your head and don't tell anyone you have it, just let it sit there in your brain, rising like dough. The truth is that the more knowledge you have, the more likely you are to make the right decision.

BURNING ZEPPELINS

Remember the girlfriends or boyfriends from hell? Remember the rubbish you put up with, remember all your dear and trusted friends saying to you: 'Leave them! Leave them! They're appalling!' and finally you do (much to everybody's relief) and another burning zeppelin goes crashing to the ground.

A work relationship is no different from any other relationship that involves other human beings. You've got to be able to recognise a wonky machine that is floating dangerously in the air when you see one. All it means is that you're on the wrong flight, there's a nut on the plane, and it might be time to bale out. But if you want to get your hands on the controls you're going to have to do it while hanging on to your self-respect, and in such a way that nobody realises exactly what you're doing. This book will help you to do just that.

If you're already in a fulfilling job and everything is going swimmingly, then you are probably aware of most of the advice contained herein. But it will still help you to get out of sticky situations and turn them to your advantage. It will help you to avoid the disaster juggernaut when it's headed in your direction. This book contains the *real* rules, which are quite different from the way people think things operate, and it will help you to keep your credibility, your self-respect and your faith in human nature intact.

three
How to survive a job you hate

'When the going gets tough, the weird turn pro.' *GONZO JOURNALIST, HUNTER S THOMPSON*

Until you can determine whether the job you have is worth keeping, you have to stay in it long enough to be able to make an informed decision about your career direction. This chapter contains some thoughts about how to assess your particular situation.

THE POISONED CHALICE

If a job starts out badly the chances are that it will become worse, not better. When you first start a new job, you should be enthusiastic and happy, full of pep and pop and vim at the thought of all the great challenges ahead of you. After a while, it should level out to a bearable routine. If you're feeling unwell in the first couple of weeks, then you may have supped from the poisoned chalice. You thought it contained the nectar of the Gods, but in fact it's bad red wine laced with arsenic. You've been misled. The company is not what you thought it was going to be; your job is totally different from what you expected.

You were amazed by your good fortune, perhaps, lured by the kudos and the money. Perhaps you did your homework but chose to ignore the company's bad reputation. Surely, it couldn't be that bad. In fact, you remarked to your friends that it was, almost, too good to be true. One thing you can be assured of is that anything that appears too good to be true, usually is.

Once you've faced up to the fact that somewhere along the line a terrible mistake was made, then you can start damage control. It's not going to get any better. Leave within three to six months. This amount of time will not cause comment on your CV and can easily be buried by the phrase 'Travelling overseas'.

IMPROVING YOUR ATTITUDE

The very first thing you have to do is get up off the couch. The trouble with misery is it's a downward spiral. Everything becomes affected: your belief in your ability, your confidence and your self-esteem. Regain some perspective: all that's happened is that you're in the wrong place with the wrong people.

Try and exercise every day; this makes you feel like you've achieved something and improves your ability to think under pressure. Try not to eat garbage: junk food makes you sluggish and stupid. Get as much sleep as you can, even though you're probably too wound up to sleep properly. There is an enlightening story concerning Winston Churchill's sleeping habits. Somebody once asked him how he could sleep when he was Prime Minister of Britain, in a time of war. His reply was: 'I get into bed. I turn off the light. I say "Bugger everybody" and I go to sleep.'

THE HALF-FULL/HALF-EMPTY SYNDROME

When people look at a glass filled with liquid, there are two responses: it is either half-full or half-empty. In your present negative state all glasses look half-empty, worse, totally empty, particularly if they were glasses of gin. You have to start looking at the situation in a more positive manner. There must be something good about it. Think carefully. Is it the view from your window of the recently completed psychiatric unit of the hospital? It looks clean and white and peaceful ... very tempting, but perhaps not quite what you're after. What about the trees? They're green and leafy. Very nice. They remind you of the trees in California, which is where you'd like to be *right now*. Are you working on a project you particularly enjoy? Enjoy it more. Do you like the ride into work? Focus on it. Do you think about lunchtime as a man dying of thirst thinks about an oasis in the desert? Finish everything you have to do with the imminent reward of a blissful half-hour or so to yourself, buried in a book. Concentrate on the other areas of your life: your friends, your hobbies, your family. Friends are particularly useful, as they can give you unbiased feedback on your current uneasy situation. Get as much joy from these things as you can. Look out the window as you're crossing the bridge or the river. Look at the sky, at the clouds. Think about all the starving children in the world. At least you're not one of *them*.

DAYDREAMING

This is not particularly recommended as a method of coping. Try and restrain yourself from looking aimlessly out the window, while your imagination runs riot with impossible dreams of your boss being arrested for drug-dealing, the company being invaded by a squad of men in suits who announce themselves as liquidators, or a group of terrorist guerrillas arriving threatening to kill you all unless your product is taken off the market. However, we do recommend that, as you struggle with insomnia, these fantasies are used instead of a sleeping draught.

The most popular fantasy of all is the resignation fantasy. Along with the fantasy itself, where you rehearse your parting words in about 100 different ways, there is the extreme satisfaction derived from actually typing it up. It brings the moment closer. Try to restrain yourself from doing this for more than five minutes per day. If you have to wean yourself off it, type up one version at the end of the day.

MENTAL HEALTH DAYS

Take these instead of sick days. Nobody in their right mind ever stays off work when they are suffering from the common cold or flu. What you actually should do is struggle valiantly through the day, a hanky held permanently to your nose. This makes you look extremely dedicated. You can then use sick days to go to the Madonna concert, enjoy a three-day party when your best friend comes back from India, sleep or work out your action plan when you are stuck in a job you hate. Take as many of these as you feel you need and do as many useful things as you can: plot your strategy, write up your CV, ring up about other positions, and go and see an agency. (In the public sector, mental health days are called stress leave. Stress leave is available in the private sector, but nobody ever takes it as it leaves everybody with the mistaken impression that you are about to enter a lunatic asylum.)

LIFE RAFT

This is a person you make friends with who is having just as bad a time as you are. With luck, there may be more than one of them. There *must* be, otherwise the problem may well be yours. Just as people who survive disasters cling together (although the ice, the sharks and a sense of despair is all they have in common) people trapped in a job they hate are an endless source of sympathy and understanding for each other. This person will keep you sane and there is no danger of boring them: they won't walk away from you, in fact your mutual stories can take the form of illuminating the big picture.

AFTERNOON COFFEE

Heartily recommended. At about three o'clock the nadir of misery is reached; it's a long time until you reach the safe haven of home, probably later than usual if you're not working up to par. Take your companion in misery away from the office and frown over your cappuccino together. It helps to break up the afternoon. Be as positive as you can about your future away from the company.

PLOTTING AND SCHEMING

This is by far the most gratifying activity. Once you have read the relevant chapters in this book, make up a list of things you can change at your work and the things you can't. Ignore the latter, and take some small steps toward improving the former. This means *everything*, even talking to the person you most hate in the office or smiling at everybody when you don't want to smile. It's going to take a lot of energy to turn the tables around to your advantage, but it gets easier as you go along.

AM I PARANOID?

A good dose of paranoia is a healthy thing. Paranoia prevents you from thinking you'll get the best from everybody all the time. It's good to hope for it — just don't expect it. Despite what you think, not *everybody* is out to get you. Just some people. This is called Facing the Facts and is very important if you are going to get ahead. Don't fool yourself into believing that everything is rosy when it quite clearly is not. Additionally, just because you think everybody thinks you're stupid, that doesn't mean you are. Don't let this kind of nibbling away at your self-esteem get to you. You know exactly what you are good at and exactly what you can do. Every day, look in the mirror and repeat to yourself all the things you are good at.

THE RULES OF SUCCESS

You may be in a difficult position at work because you broke several of these major rules. These are the ultimate rules of 'getting along' and since the major source of problems at work has to do with people, rather than corporate structure or professional competence, then it's a good idea to learn them. Ignore them at your peril.

- Don't imbibe to excess. You can drink as many vodka, lime and sodas as your stomach can stand: just don't add the vodka. It's hard to be taken seriously when your speech is muffled due to the fact that your head is buried in the carpet.
- Don't wear inappropriate clothes. Unless they're part of your uniform, jeans should never be worn. It looks like you didn't think about it before you got dressed. Conversely, don't wear a suit when it's civvies day: people will think you're a nerd.
- Don't say bitchy things about anybody, ever. All that will happen is that they'll be repeated to the person. This is fine if you want to float a false rumour, but you'll soon get a reputation for flapping gums and nobody will tell you anything.
- Don't eat all the scotch fingers or chocolate chip cookies in the biscuit tin.

- Don't criticise the company while you are in the office. Office walls are paper thin, and while you're on the phone to your mate, whingeing about the incompetent fool in accounts, somebody may well have their ear mashed up against it. Also, don't use the computer or fax to write denigrating letters and don't give your e-mail password to anybody. Sadly, these modern-day bits of technology have memories.
- Don't leave your coffee cup for somebody else to wash. Grown women have been reduced to tears over this.
- Greet everybody with 'Good morning'. No matter how late you arrive, people will remember you're there. Also make the odd attempt to work later than everybody else (even just ten minutes), then you can say you worked until eight o'clock and nobody will know the difference.
- Don't sleep with work colleagues.
- Remember all birthdays. An inexpensive bunch of flowers goes down well. Also the odd tray of homemade lammies or chocolate crackles (buy them if you have to) will sweeten any dodgy opinions.
- Always ask advice and opinions from others. Even if you already know the answers, people love to be asked their opinion.
- Don't cry, ever. If you are a woman, this is fatal: people will think you're a wimp. For a man, it is a better option to jump out the window. There are no circumstances under which it is acceptable. Howl as much as you like at home, that's what it's there for.
- Never win a fight with your boss. Not many of us can actually manage this. If you are so stupid as to be engaged in a dispute with your boss then try to lose it, with dignity. Bosses do not like to have mistakes pointed out to them and do not like to be backed into a corner. Once

cornered, they will lash out at you tooth and claw. And they will win. That is how they got to be the boss in the first place.

- Never talk about your personal life. This will be used against you at a later stage if it isn't going well, as in 'He/she has personal problems, poor thing'. Confine yourself to comments like 'Went sailing' when people ask what you did on the weekend, even though you and your partner had a huge fight which culminated in you throwing his/her stuff in a magnificent pile on the front lawn.

- Never pretend to know more than you do. All that will happen is that you will end up knowing nothing at all. It is not humanly possible for everybody to know everything about anything. If you don't know something, don't be afraid of asking. You'll learn more and get things done more quickly.

- Trust nobody. Pay no attention to what people say, it's all irrelevant anyway. How many times have we said 'I love you' to somebody, when we don't? Instead, pay attention to what they *do*. Observe everything and everybody. By doing this, you will soon know the few precious people who can be trusted and how much you can trust them with. But remember, at the end of the day, you never know who is squeezing whom, so be careful.

True Crimes — Real Life Story

Working as a print journalist when computers were introduced, Susan learned a valuable lesson about taking new technology for granted. Her publishing company installed VDTs (Video Display Terminals) for every employee, to be used by journalists to type their stories directly onto the system, instead of going through the laborious process of the old, typewritten method. Typing directly onto the system, the copy could then be accessed by the subeditors, who edited it and sent it electronically to page layout.

Susan was unfamiliar with the new technology and, while waiting for people to return phone calls, she wrote a letter to a friend using the system. Her opening paragraph contained the momentous news of the past months: she was no longer celibate. Her first line ran as follows with a newsy feel: 'STOP PRESS! STOP PRESS! Last night, Susan Cartwell of 59 Johnson Street, Maidstone, had a f—k!' Following this were all the gory details of the encounter in startling clarity.

Thinking nothing more of it, Susan printed out the letter and mailed it. The next day, she was horrified to discover, through a warning phone call from a friendly soul, that her letter had been sent, via computer, to every news bureau in the country. Susan was unaware of one crucial fact: anything she typed onto the VDT was automatically saved and accessible to the subeditors, who were obviously unable to resist such a God-sent opportunity.

Arthur C. Clarke didn't invent HAL 9000 the evil computer for no reason at all. Susan was infected by the lethal computer virus VDT (Very Dangerous Talking) and the moral of this story is obvious: beware of new technology.

New kid on the block

four — the basics

'I don't think people think of work as a workplace. I think they think of it as a stationery store with Danish.' *JERRY SEINFELD*

Whether you have just arrived at your first job or have moved to a new one, your initial reactions will probably be much the same. Who are all these people? What do they do? What on earth are they talking about? It's as if you've just been beamed up from the Enterprise and have materialised in this alien environment. It might be worthwhile taking a leaf out of Captain Kirk and Spock's book. What is the first thing they do when they are placed in an unfamiliar environment? They do three things: keep their mouths shut, view everybody with suspicion and try to appear as inconspicuous as possible before they take any action. Of course, their silly clothes don't really assist them in this last endeavour, which is another point to bear in mind during your first few weeks. In the end, this forbearance makes sure that they succeed in their mission — as you will too, if you play it smart.

At a rough estimate, it will take you about six months to feel comfortable; three if you're a fast learner. There are several important things that you must do before you can really begin to function efficiently in your job. They are as follows: find out who everybody is and what they do. Find out who really has the power and who just pretends to. Find out who is going to impinge on your position and either assist or impede it. Find out who can be trusted and who cannot. The point of all this information is to protect your future: once you know what other people are doing and why they are doing it, you can put people in two camps: people who will help you and people who won't.

There are two major areas to familiarise yourself with when you first start working: the corporate structure and the corporate culture. Briefly, the corporate structure tells you who's got the power on paper and the corporate culture tells you who's got the power in reality and what's acceptable as far as dress, social occasions and conversation go. We'll discuss both of them in this chapter.

CORPORATE STRUCTURE

It's important that you know how the company operates on paper. In existence there should be a plan or structure which shows where each person sits in relation to everybody else. It's rather like a genealogical chart, which shows you how you are related to your loopy old Uncle Billy who bit you the last time you saw him.

Most companies are a pyramid, with one person sitting at the top. Underneath the apex the pyramid gets fatter gradually, with minions a large bunch at the bottom. (Some companies can operate as upside-down pyramids with about a thousand chiefs with long, impressive titles, and not many Indians to do all the work. This is not a good company to work for, as the politics of struggle prevent any real work being done.)

You can usually tell who is getting close to the top of the pyramid by the size of the office they work in. Managing directors have enormous offices usually, designed to cow and intimidate you as they glare at you from the other end of an enormous expanse of polished table. In the next rank down are the understudies. They are waiting for the MD to get hit by a bus, then they can fill their God-given place on the stage. The infighting can get pretty vicious at this level, as there ain't enough room for all of them at the top of that little pyramid. Their offices are usually smaller versions of the MD's office, and sometimes, they lock them ostentatiously as they leave. The MD never locks his/her office, usually because there's nothing important in it except the drinks bar, and that has its own lock. He doesn't bother cluttering up his space with bits of paper — that's for somebody else to worry about.

The next rank down consists of middle management types. At this level, it is a real free-for-all. They've got a long way to go to get closer to the top of the pyramid and they have to make sure they're one of the few chosen to be elevated. Middle managers tend to have the most responsibility and therefore work the hardest — they have to, to survive. It's no surprise that they have to elbow a few people off the pyramid as they go higher up.

The offices of middle management are crowded with files and there's barely room for a visitor's chair, causing them to indulge in a popular game called 'counting the squares'. This means they count the number of ceiling squares in their office, and then everybody else's, to see whether other people have got a bigger office than they do. If somebody does have more ceiling squares, they instantly fall into a deep depression, as a bigger office usually means, in this paranoid atmosphere, closer proximity to the giant office currently inhabited by the managing director. It's like being a Catholic and being given a 'sign' of your vocation to enter the Church. The more office squares, the bigger the sign. (A window, or a 'view', operates in the same way.)

Following middle management are a range of assistants, coordinators, administrators, gofers and so on. They live in small boxes crowded around the interior of the office, like battery chickens. They don't really care about anybody else as they're much too concerned about managing the job at hand and paying all their bills in the lunch hour.

Chain-of-command

The above-mentioned chart will help you to map your progress through the organisation. (If the company doesn't have one, don't take the job: it will be an unmitigated disaster.) Look at this chart very carefully and find out, on paper, who your boss is and who their boss is. Find out who has nothing whatsoever to do with you. Very often, the person who has nothing whatsoever to do with you on paper, is the person who is continually telling you to do things. This is where you can use the paper to protect yourself, by telling your boss that this person has no control over you and showing them the bit of paper on which is printed the company structure. This should fix them and they will then only be allowed to tell you what to do by a special dispensation: a memo written by your boss, their boss and everybody else outlining exactly what you have to do and when you have to do it by.

Direct report — keeping Dick or Jane happy

The chart will show you exactly who you report to. This person is your direct report who will have the ultimate power over you, body and soul, while you are at work. Whether named Dick or Jane, your DR is your number one priority, the person you have to keep happy at all costs. Your number two priority is your DR's DR. Ignore people from other divisions who have no say over your hiring, firing or pay packet.

Follow the line through the chart and you will see that, as all roads lead to Rome, so all roads lead to one person: the managing director. Note all the people along the way, because these people you may encounter if anything goes wrong. Following the chain-of-command is called *procedure* and it must be followed if you are to protect yourself. If something goes wrong with your relationship with your boss, you can't just go barging into the MD's office, complaining loudly.

What you have to do is go to his/her boss. This is called 'going over their head' and is not done for any trivial reason. It's usually done when you have received anything in writing that can be construed as a warning or a prelude to the attitude speech. You can move up the line, or you can move sideways, if your boss's direct report is as bad as he/she is, and talk to a more sympathetic person who, though from another division, is still in senior management. Remember, there's a lot of elbowing going on at this level, though the ranks have thinned out a lot, and everybody is looking for an opportunity to shaft somebody else. When you 'go over their head' choose the person wisely if you want to achieve your aim.

Job description

Upon entering the company, you should have a job description, outlining who you report to and what you have to do to earn that magnificent pay packet every week. It is very, very bad if you do not have one of these because it means that your job can change, chameleon-like, and before you know it you'll be delivering the mail. Insist on getting one of these before you take the position, indeed, at the interview.

You can use this piece of paper to hide behind. If it isn't in your job description, a special dispensation can again be granted. (You may also ask for some compensation for doing this special task, but before you do be careful that it doesn't come under the clause at the end of every well-written job description entitled: 'Other projects as necessary at the discretion of the Managing Director'.) Any changes to your job description will have to be discussed and then added to the written paper already in existence. Think carefully before agreeing to anything. If it becomes a totally different job, then it's not the job you were hired to do, is it?

Federal and state industrial awards

These are government regulations which show you how much money you should be making and detail things like working hours and conditions. About 75 per cent of Australians come under some sort of industrial award (the remaining 25 per cent are covered by contracts of some kind: either verbal or written) but it is not as simple as it seems. You may come under a federal award or a state award.

The onus is on the employer to tell you what award you come under but often, as we know, some employers are a bit slack in this area. All Commonwealth public service employees come under the Australian Public Service Award (except for statutory authorities) and are bound by the Australian *Public Service Act 1922*; they are told automatically as part of their induction what award they come under, but for state government public servants and private enterprise employees the situation is a little different. Being paranoid, even if you only ask what award you come under, you may find they look at you suspiciously and think you are a 'troublemaker'. The last thing any company wants is intervention or trouble from government authorities or unions.

Find out what award you come under by approaching, firstly, your pay office. If people look at you with suspicion, try ringing the Department of Industrial Relations in your state, or the federal department, which handles over 3000 awards and 4000 enterprise agreements. (An enterprise agreement is an agreement whereby special work conditions are agreed to by the employer, the employee and the union that bypass the award under which the employee is operating. This is mainly the case in Victoria where industrial awards, in the main, have been abolished.) They will tell you if you come under a federal or state award. Also note that all state awards may differ even if they are called the same thing. For instance, you may be under a certain set of conditions under the Hotels Award in New South Wales, and under a completely different set of conditions in Queensland.

Once you've found out what award you are under, you can then determine if the employer is meeting the conditions of that award. Most employers are reasonable and if you're happy and they're happy, then everything should be fine, but it is useful to know if they haven't met conditions of the award in case further action is required by you at some later date.

If you are not a member of a union, the Department of Industrial Relations (DIR) will investigate your complaint and declare the employer in breach of the award. If the employer discovers you are talking to the DIR, and they sack you, you can then lodge a complaint of 'unfair dismissal' with them in which you can seek monetary compensation and/or reinstatement. Contact numbers for the DIR in each state are listed in 'People who can help you' at the back of the book.

Union action

Just because you are covered by an award does not mean you necessarily belong to a union. Unions are the one thing employers will not tell you about. (If you work for the public service at the Commonwealth level, you automatically come under the CPSU — Community and Public Sector Union.) If you are a public servant for a state government, you may come under various awards and unions. If you do not know what union you should belong to, then try ringing the labour council in your state. See the section 'People who can help you' for phone numbers.

If you are having trouble with your employer, your union is the first body you should talk to. It is important that unions exist, particularly if you have no other form of redress. If you have a legitimate complaint but are receiving no support or advice from inside the organisation, then you will need to go outside for this — and that is where your union comes in. Some unions will give you advice over the phone even if you don't belong, but mostly they will want you to join before they begin helping you.

If you are required to do something at your work where you feel you need some legal advice very quickly (e.g. if you are required to sign a piece of paper by five o'clock) then you may want to get some legal advice from a good law firm. Find a law firm that specialises in labour law as the laws are extremely complicated, ever-changing and you need to consult professionals who know their way around the traps. To find a law firm that specialises in labour law, ring the Law Institute or Law Society in your state.

Government policy

The Australian Commonwealth public sector is bound by the *Public Service Act 1922* which gives guidelines on official conduct of public servants, who must:

- Be responsive to the government of the day and impartial in carrying out their decisions.
- Be accountable for their actions.
- Be responsive to the public.
- Make fair and equitable decisions.
- Work professionally with skill, care, diligence and impartiality.
- Avoid conflicts of interest between their personal life and official duties.
- Ensure non-disclosure of official information unless in the course of their duties.
- Not use their position to influence a person.
- Not use their official position to obtain gifts and other benefits.

If public servants feel that corruption is taking place then they can refer the matter to the ICAC (Independent Commission Against Corruption), which exists to prevent and take legal action against wrongdoings in the public sector (only in New South Wales). Unfortunately, no such body exists for private enterprise, where you have to be a lot cleverer, and nastier, to make your point.

Sexual harassment

There is legislation (the *Sex Discrimination Act 1984*) to protect you if you feel you are being sexually harassed, but political correctness has made major inroads into this area at work.

During our lives, we all have to deal with unwanted sexual advances from people and it's a good idea to start dealing with them sooner than later and not crying 'sexual harassment' every time somebody asks you to have a look at their etchings. For a start, it worries you unnecessarily and is a big waste of a lot of people's time and money. One should be able to extricate oneself from these situations with grace and style.

Sexual harassment is a major issue when you are in danger of losing your job because of it. For this reason, harassment usually happens from a superior downwards; a dumb pass from the mail boy is just that — after all, what's the most he can do to you, not deliver your mail? Work and even the law do not change people's basic personalities. If you think somebody is cute, sometimes you can't stop yourself from imagining them stretched out on your sheets, and before you know it you've had a couple of drinks and made an idiotic pass. It's the 'I might get lucky' syndrome. Make enough dumb passes and, sooner or later, somebody's bound to say 'yes'. Real sexual harassment is repetitive, making you feel that if you reject these advances your life will be made miserable or your career will be hampered, or you may even get the sack. Say you're at a company dinner, your boss is a man, and you feel a pressure on your leg. You know that it isn't water on the knee caused by playing too much netball but your boss's hand — you've got to think quickly.

If you like him, well, you can try taking his hand. Hey! there's no law against it, but bear in mind you will be breaking one of the major rules of success at work and possibly opening yourself up to all sorts of nasty allegations and consequences. Like I said, do what you want, just be aware of what may happen if you do.

If you don't want his hand to be there you can do a number of things depending on the kind of person he is. You can ignore it. (This is often most effective, as the hand is quietly withdrawn and the incident never mentioned again.) You can say, quietly 'Please take your hand off my knee, I don't like it'. You can say 'What is this doing on my knee?' bring it out in front of everybody and wave it about. You can do a number of things, but it isn't necessary, at this stage, to bring a charge of sexual harassment.

You've got to make it quite clear at the outset what the story is. Words to the effect of 'Never in your wildest dreams, buddy. Even if I was dead, I'd complain. Don't even think about it!' can get the message across nicely. But sitting there and fluttering your eyelashes and smiling because you don't know what else to do can be interpreted as encouragement by some dim, or drunk, people.

If the incident happens again there's a good chance the person didn't hear you properly the first time, wasn't listening to you at all, couldn't hear you over the noise of the band or is just an idiot. Some people are, you know. This is the time when you say 'Listen. You're sailing pretty close to the wind on a sexual harassment charge. I'd give up while the going's good' or some such thing.

If it continues and you feel your livelihood is threatened, then you should first contact your union, or the Human Rights and Equal Opportunity Commission in your state (contact numbers are listed at the back of the book in 'People who can help you').

True Crimes — Real Life Story

'Our boss was a maniac,' says Mary. 'Wasn't he?' She looks for confirmation to her former work colleague, Yolande.

'Yep,' Yolande agrees. 'He was a maniac. The thing to remember about our story,' she continues, 'is that there are two kinds of harassment: sexual and professional. There was no doubt that our boss sexually harassed us, but by far the most important issue, as far as we were concerned, was the fact that he professionally harassed us as well. And we knew that this was going to cause us far more trouble than anything else.'

Yolande and Mary's boss, the administration manager, was a man with no purpose, no reason for being, no idea. He seemed to exist in a void, a soulless universe peopled by his own fantasies. He should have been, as they said 'locked up'. He was a person of whom people said 'He has a lot of problems at home'. Yolande and Mary never knew what was going to happen from one moment to the next. One day he was all chummy with them, the next day he acted like they didn't exist. He had a particularly nasty habit of telling the two what to do, and then subsequently changing his mind. He would then write a memo, changing his story on paper, implying that one or both of them had deliberately disobeyed him.

'All of his memos looked like warning memos. Because he was a terrible communicator, you never knew when you might find one of these nasty little epistles on your desk when you walked in,' says Mary. 'On the odd occasion when I challenged him, he had a very off-putting way of responding. He would come up to me, put his arms around my neck and kiss me on the cheek. He would whisper: "There! We're all friends now!"'

'He used to call me "cup-cake",' interjects Yolande, witheringly. 'He used to walk in and say, cheerily: "Good morning, cup-cake!" I used to think to myself, "Am I wearing a cherry for a hat?"'

'Finally, the two of us received a joint memo,' says Mary. 'It was the weirdest memo, like something a schoolmaster writes to a naughty student. We were not "now allowed" to do this, we were not "now privileged" to be doing that. It was quite obviously the work of a madman.'

Yolande decided to take issue with the memo as it was quite clearly, as she said, a go-for-broke warning memo. Their boss was away at a conference when they decided to take action and the managing director was overseas. Very cleverly, they decided to approach a female senior manager in the company.

'The very first thing we did was go to see our union,' says Yolande. 'We made up some weak excuse why we had the time off and, of course, we had to join, but it was worth it. We discovered that there had been numerous complaints after the fact against this man that the union was aware of, but nobody had yet taken any action.'

'Well, they couldn't really take any action,' she finishes ruefully, 'they'd all been sacked before they got a chance.'

'The next thing we did,' says Mary, 'was to write up an agenda of points we wanted to discuss with the senior female manager and ambushed her. We didn't put sexual harassment on the agenda (professional harassment was the main item) but we mentioned it to her. Her eyebrows went right up into her hair, she was so surprised. Our sexual harassment was our "ace in the hole" so to speak. We weren't going to use it unless we were really pushed and then it would have been all the way. We also mentioned that we had "received legal advice from our union".'

'All kinds of odd things happened next,' says Yolande, 'which confirmed that we weren't imagining the severity of the situation. Several other senior managers approached us in the street, or in the park across the road from the office, saying that we had done the right thing. Naturally, this didn't translate into real support at any level in the office, but they were quite happy that we were taking him on. In that respect they were all accountable as well as being gutless as hell.

'The next thing that happened was a nervous interstate telephone call from our boss,' continues Yolande. 'I took the call and told him that as I was seeking "legal advice" it was not in my interests to talk to him.'

This dynamite duo were extremely smart: by taking such serious charges to another senior manager they ensured that action had to be taken. Nobody could hide it under the carpet. It was fortuitous that the managing director was away, as no real, serious action against the women (like instant dismissal on some trumped-up charge) could be taken unless he was there.

When he returned, a meeting was called. The female senior manager had 'warned' him that the two had received legal advice. This effectively stymied him, as he realised he could not sack them, unless he wanted to be involved in a lengthy and expensive court case.

'We had a long meeting,' says Mary, 'which involved both the managing director and our boss. In it we insisted that we receive written apologies for the appalling memo. We tried for other things, like reporting to a higher authority, but we had to negotiate.'

'The whole meeting was minuted by the managing director,' says Yolande, 'which was a complete joke. Everybody knows that unless there's an independent observer to take minutes, people can challenge anything that happened in the meeting. We had to sign the managing director's version of the meeting but we didn't do that until some changes were made to the document. Whole sections of what we knew had occurred just hadn't been put in! If it was designed for their legal protection it wasn't even worth the paper it was written on. It would have been laughed out of court.

'As soon as I saw the MD taking the minutes, I knew we were dealing with a pack of charlies with no idea.'

'It was awful while it was happening,' says Mary. 'I couldn't bear to talk to my boss, he scared me so much. But Yolande said to keep my head up, look everybody in the eye and never let anybody know how much they got to us. And she was right. That is the only way to behave in a situation like that.'

The women received a written apology from their boss and an assurance from the managing director that he would closely follow the department, and support a slight restructure, regular meetings and so on.

'We naturally knew that the whole thing was a pack of nonsense,' says Mary. 'I think our boss turned over a new leaf for about 24 hours, then he just reverted to his old bad habits. We were still considering union involvement, but we knew that we would never work again in our industry, it was so small. Eventually, I left, to a better job with a more professional company. I had been with the company for only four months.'

'I stayed on for another few months,' says Yolande, 'but it was unbearable. He was more unstable than ever. Eventually, I just resigned and on the very day I was leaving, I was offered another job, the job that I wanted. When I resigned I told the managing director I thought my boss was "psychotic" and that he should be committed. In reply, he said to me: "He's a difficult person to work with" and I said: "No. Anybody without a grain of self-respect can work for him. Anybody without a personality or a spine." I was so glad I said that.'

By calculating the right person to talk to, following procedure and not panicking, Yolande and Mary achieved what they wanted: they maintained their reputations and continued their careers in the same industry. When asked what had happened at the company, both replied that they had found 'that they had not effectively used their talents or skills in the job', but behind the scenes and confidentially, they disclosed that the real reason was sexual and professional harassment. Together they did more damage to their boss's reputation than he would have imagined possible. A year after these events took place, their boss 'resigned' and has been unable to find work in the same industry again.

Discrimination

Discrimination can happen in various forms at work and legislation is in place to prevent it. Discrimination can occur because of sex, pregnancy, race, colour, nationality, ethnic or ethno-religious background, marital status, physical or intellectual disability, homosexuality or age. Once again, you've got to make sure you don't have the wrong end of the stick. Some people are constantly whingeing about 'discrimination' towards them, when the real reason they're constantly being pulled up in performance reviews is because they are lazy and incompetent, not because they come from another country. Stupidity, laziness, greed and nastiness seem to cross all cultural barriers and do not confine themselves to one set of people.

If you feel that you have a legitimate case for alleging that you have suffered discrimination, contact your union first, or the Human Rights and Equal Opportunity Commission in your state (see 'People who can help you', at the back of the book).

By far the best thing you can do if you're in trouble is to talk to your union. Its industrial officers know the best way of approaching the situation for your ultimate good. Always remember that you are in control. Some unions are just dying to get into places, boots and all, which may be very worthy, but not good for your career in the long term. Use them as far as you need them, but never let them push you into a situation where you feel your long-term career reputation may be at risk.

PLAYING HAPPY FAMILIES — THE CORPORATE CULTURE

Unlike popular culture, in which a ground swell of popular opinion can change things, everything in the work environment comes from the top down. Whatever goes on does so with either the tacit acceptance or active participation of management.

Understanding the corporate culture means that you won't stuff up by swimming against the current. Even if you hate being called away from your desk for another boring (and fattening) morning tea which takes up one hour of precious time, there's no point in whingeing about it. Just eat a pikelet, smile and keep your mouth shut. Not participating means you don't like them, and soon they'll turn that around so that *they* don't like *you*.

The laid-back company

Everybody here wears jeans or some young designer variation thereof. They use words like 'cool', 'great' and 'man'. On Melbourne Cup Day they wear no hats but consume immense quantities of good champagne and listen to Roy and HG for the race call. The company is usually in advertising, magazine publishing, design, entertainment, hospitality, or is a hip computer company. Birthdays, lunches and resignations are celebrated by a long lunch after which the boss pays, but for this largesse they expect their pound of flesh. People work to intense deadlines so there are periods of frenetic activity, in which everybody works 14-hour days for a period, followed by a lull of long, boozy lunches, late arrivals and early departures.

Conversation is about films, magazines, music and popular culture, but beware: there's cool popular culture (*Ren & Stimpy*) and then square popular culture (*Melrose Place*).

The snap and scrabble company

These employees like to think they're cool but they're not. Dress is on the knife edge of fashion but it's the blunt edge. There's a mixture of jeans, body shirts and jackets, with the regular designer-suit-with-a-difference for women, and baggy pants, baggy shirt and floral tie for the men (Italian shoes an optional extra). Key words here are 'great' and 'fine' and 'good': familiarity with a familial tone.

On Melbourne Cup Day they all wear silly hats, a prize is given for the silliest, and they talk all through the race. The company is usually in sales, book publishing, public relations, human resources, or perhaps in investment or telemarketing. The hours are usually long and long lunches are frowned upon. Every quarter or six months people are taken out for lunch. Group activities outside of work hours are favoured, such as sales conferences or long work dinners on a Friday night. Conversation consists of discussing the latest episode of a popular television series and what the last edition of *Cosmopolitan* said about The Other Woman. Humour may be of the scatological/slapstick variety. When people leave they are either taken out to lunch by their supervisor for one and a half hours exactly or they are subjected to an antiquated practice known as a 'morning tea', during which a watchful eye is kept on all employees as they consume pikelets, scones and particularly cloying little cakes known as neenish tarts. It's true the company pays, but they don't want to pay that much: they're paying you already, aren't they?

The bottom line company

This sort of company is intensely serious and focused. It is usually in accountancy, finance, banking, engineering, computers, law or practically any variety of profession you can name. Their words are precise: 'yes' and 'no' and 'I don't feel that's appropriate' are virtually the only sounds you will hear, apart from the clicking of calculators. Dress is serious and conservative; even now it may be unusual for women to wear pants, while men favour the regulation blue or grey suit. On Melbourne Cup Day they stop operating for the exact time of the race, turning the television on when it starts and off when it stops. Needless to say, they wear no hats at all.

People come in at 8.00 am and leave at 6.00 pm, unless it's budget night or a major share offer, in which case they stay up all night. They usually have an active social club which throws a few beers and wine on at 5.30 on a Friday night. Additionally, they have membership in several professional societies, and there is an annual dinner at which everybody gets totally plastered and turns up the next morning at the unheard of hour of 10.00 am still wearing their dinner suit and the remains of the evening dress.

The el cheapo company

Its management hate spending money. They resent you because they have to pay your wages, and usually endeavour to underpay you or overtax you. These are usually service or hospitality companies, or small businesses of any variety. Phrases such as 'There's a nice recipe in here for chicken schnitzel' are heard. Serious discussions about the 'personalities' of various television characters, spoken of in reverent tones as if the characters were real people, are also conducted. Other topics of conversation may include personal grooming (as in 'Oh no! I broke a nail') or 'I don't know what we're going to do, business is down'. These comments are designed to instil in you a constant state of insecurity and a desire for permanent domicile in a cave in Tasmania. If you turn up ten minutes early they won't pay you, but if you turn up ten minutes late, they will dock your pay.

Melbourne Cup Day comes . . . and Melbourne Cup Day goes. At some fortunate places, you may listen to it on the radio. On your birthday, you will be given a card encrusted with the appropriate sentiments. The only thing the boss cannot escape is the Christmas party. If more generous, he will take you to lunch at the pub, but otherwise the festivities are usually confined to a lukewarm bottle of champagne after all the cleaning up has been done.

The public sector

This is the Culture of Paranoia. They hate spending money but that's because it's the taxpayers' money. Every cent has to be accounted for and lunches, dinners and other perks just cannot be explained away satisfactorily. They have therefore instituted a more civilised form of the morning tea: a cake is whipped out for every birthday, resignation, retirement, birth, pregnancy, engagement, marriage, holiday, death or funeral. Any excuse will do, and some departments have two or three of these a week. The cake is bought on a round-robin basis and the eating of it constitutes about half an hour of precious taxpaying time.

For major occasions like Christmas and Melbourne Cup Day there is either a lunch, at which everybody pays for themselves, or a picnic or barbeque-type event where everybody brings a plate and makes earnest small talk on the side of a windy hillside unrelieved by alcohol, which, if it flows, flows like treacle. They all trudge home, dead sober, at the merciful end of the day.

Government offices have things like flexitime and flexi-days, which they all scrupulously observe. Part of the reason why government departments operate at the speed of a snail is because they are given nothing to relieve the psychological burden of 'looking after the people's money'. It is considered somewhat more vocational than a regular job.

WHO'S WHO

This will get you a long way. There are three very important people in any organisation: the receptionist, the boss's assistant and the boss's confidante. The former two are, usually, women, and although they do not appear to have much power, in fact they have a great deal.

Receptionists are a great source of information for simple things like where people are going and what they are doing. They know who is talking to whom. They know what time people get in to work and, usually, what time they leave. They know everybody and, from this information, they have some very useful opinions about people. There are people they like and people they loathe. They are often correct in their opinions: people who treat receptionists badly simply because they are in a subordinate position to themselves may well do the same to you.

Bosses' assistants know their boss's opinions on a variety of information as well as heaps of confidential information, some of which sumptuous details they may leak to you if you get them in the right mood.

The boss's confidante could be anybody in the organisation, but is usually somebody on the same level or just beneath. This person is usually the one the boss leaves in charge when he/she goes away. (In lots of cases that is the financial controller.) They are widely believed to be understudying the position of boss and will eventually get on stage if one day the boss doesn't turn up.

THE 9 TO 5 MYTH

This is a commonly held fiction. Rarely do most people put in their regulation 7.5 hours a day, unless they work in manufacturing. You will soon discover that all you have to do is show up and you can actually do the real work in about three hours. The rest of the time is spent either enabling projects to get under way, or maintaining your position, fighting off threats and making allies or enemies. It's called 'schmoozing'.

It's actually quite easy to get to know people in a work situation: just be extremely nice, all the time. You should not be in your office much in your first weeks; you've got to be out and about schmoozing. All these people you see apparently not working and leaning on people's desks are working. They are putting in their regulation schmoozing hours.

SUSSING OUT OTHER PEOPLE'S AGENDAS

You probably know your own reasons for working; now you have to find out what motivates other people. Are they working for power, money or prestige? Are they jealous, greedy, fair, just or selfish? Can you trust them? Can they trust you? This is essential information as it will enable you to work out who to avoid and who to cultivate and where people will stand if the snowball of disaster starts rolling.

In your first few weeks you will want to be known for your friendly smile and reserved demeanour. While you are smiling and nodding, talk to everybody. Start off by asking them how their weekend was. If they mention their sister or their mother, ask about them. Try and engage them in the kind of conversation where they bring you into their confidence. In return, throw in a couple of insignificant confidences of your own. Then, gradually, ask each of them to lunch or afternoon coffee. You'll have to pay for this, but it's money well spent. It's truly enlightening what people will tell you in a one-on-one situation, particularly when you are paying.

True Crimes — Real Life Story

Michael, a 31-year-old investment adviser, recently moved companies to work in a prestigious international investment bank in a senior position. Young and talented, he was brought in as part of a management restructuring scheme which focused on younger people to deal with younger, entrepreneurial clients.

'I knew there was going to be a lot of resentment towards me when I first started in the job,' he says. 'There had been a lot of retrenchments: everybody was in a nervous state and were worried that their jobs were on the line. Investment banking is a conservative industry: I was seen as an "upstart" with big ideas.

'I knew it was going to be an uphill struggle. My first couple of months were difficult: I had to get on top of the job as well as get people to work with me instead of opposing me. I was doing no work during the day and was working until midnight most nights. My partner was really impressed!

'In my first weeks I took everybody out to lunch. These lunches went on for hours sometimes. It was the smartest thing I ever did. People relax when they're not in the office. All I did was ask questions about the company, their perceived position, their gripes, what they did on the weekend. I made no judgments — all I did was nod and smile. It's amazing what people will tell you if you ask them a direct question. Before I knew it, I knew why they were angry and resentful. Best of all, by taking me into their confidence, they perceived me as a friend, not an enemy.

'Of course, there were some people who didn't tell me a thing. But that, in itself, told me something. I have since found them the most difficult to work with. Unfortunately, a lot of them have since left the organisation because they couldn't manage the changes.'

True Crimes — Real Life Story

Jonathon lost his job because of his inability to believe that people will do anything to protect their power base. He had worked hard for his position as nurse educator at a variety of hospitals, had done his degree and gradually moved up through the ranks to a position in the health care industry responsible for blood collection, dispensing and research.

'I discovered, during my first weeks, that my work colleagues absolutely hated me,' says Jonathon. 'This surprised me initially, as I tend to believe the best of people and I always think they will behave in a reasonable manner.'

Jonathon's hopes for the position took a swan dive when he realised he had stumbled into a corporate culture that was based on paranoia. As career public servants in the health care industry, used to a 'closed circle' of women and friends with whom they had worked for years, they were being threatened by a restructure along with new management that threatened their power base and careers. They viewed Jonathon as the first element of drastic change that was coming their way and reacted in as defensive a manner as possible: cutting him out from the information circle almost from the beginning, springing surprise meetings on him, and attacking him using emotional terms at every opportunity.

'At first, I didn't realise what was going on. The person with whom I worked most closely proved to be very good friends with senior management. She was a difficult person. It wasn't until later, after a number of incidents where I had been blamed for her mistakes, that I realised she was actually a spy sent down by senior management [whom Jonathon now refers to as 'a closed circle of old witches standing around a steaming cauldron'] to discredit me and hopefully, wear me down until I resigned.

'The woman was weird,' he says. 'Weird. She was in her late thirties and desperate, without a man in sight. So she fixated on me. I ain't no prize pig as people will tell you, but she thought I was wonderful. She used to send cards to my house. I still have them, all of them. If we had a professional disagreement, a few days later I would find a little love-note in my letterbox full of profuse apologies and purple prose. I was not interested in her the slightest.

'When I rejected these advances, she became a viper and proceeded to undermine me within her little circle of power-holders.

'I was responsible for accrediting mobile and country units. She (The Weirdo) was responsible for the metropolitan side of things. This was a huge, ramshackle, outdated and outmoded institution that needed bringing into the twentieth century. Because of this, all the regional and mobile units had their own way of doing things. My method of bringing them into line training-wise was to introduce them to the concept at first and let them work their way around it, before I started laying down hard and fast rules. It was a long-term process that was going to take a couple of years at least.

'The Weirdo had written a training program that she used for metropolitan units, but I didn't think it was appropriate for the regional areas to use this, so I didn't send it to them. So, I went out there one day and found a regional unit looking at the stuff that had been sent down from head office (obviously from The Weirdo) that I didn't even know about! I was furious! This was not the way I felt it was best to proceed. I didn't say anything and roared back to head office in a condition known as dudgeon.

'When I got there I found myself ambushed in a disciplinary meeting. People talk about men's clubs, but women are just as bad. These women were like the Furies, saying that I had said that head office was useless and that I had said The Weirdo's manual wasn't worth the paper it was written on — none of which I'd said. Besides which, you can't really discipline anybody for things they have allegedly said — only for outright acts of incompetence and in the public sector even that's pretty difficult. It was the most obvious case of unfair dealing I have ever seen in my working life so far.

'They had me on the ropes — I was on a knife edge to either quitting through frustration or being shoved out. Then, finally, somebody from the regional mobile unit rang through to the Director and said that she had said all those critical things about head office, that it wasn't me and that I had been perfectly professional.

'They had to leave me alone after that, but they continued to make my life difficult in similar ways until I left. My God, I've never seen anything like it. There was no such thing as professionalism: they behaved like a bunch of conservative old biddies gossiping over an apple tea-cake, using telephone calls and alleged conversations and what so-and-so said to such-and-such to justify a disciplinary interview! Amazing!'

This nasty little anecdote is a classic case of ambush and unprofessional dealing. Think carefully about taking any job dominated by either sex. Both groups operate in exactly the same way: they protect their power structure against any outsider. It's a phenomenon that happens in social circles too, where jargon, inside jokes and isolation are used to make the person feel excluded.

TRUST

Ever heard somebody say: 'I don't like him. Don't trust the bastard'? Trust is the foundation stone of any successful relationship but establishing it is not an easy thing to do; in some friendships it can take years.

Your trust should be held in your company, your boss and yourself. You trust that they meant what they said in the interview, that they believe in your abilities and that they will let you alone to do the job. From the employer point of view, they need to be reassured that you are everything you said you were in the interview.

Once trust breaks down, you will find that your willingness to work starts cracking at the edges. If you no longer believe what your company says is true, if you believe that not only have they been lying to other people but to their employees too, then trust is broken. A breach of trust can result from simple things like managers assuring you that they treat everybody equally and fairly, when you can see quite clearly that they have distinct favourites who are not subject to the same rules as everybody else. (We are not referring to senior management: they are often treated differently for the simple reason that they have more responsibility and more pressure.)

Trust is a valuable quality and should not be underrated. Cynically, it means that you will often know things that other people don't, simply because you can keep them to yourself. Trust is a good thing to establish with other people and will help you to turn what you say into what you do. If you say you will have that report done by a certain date, then you'd better deliver, otherwise people will view your deadlines with suspicion. In such circumstances, trust is eroded.

Trust in yourself is paramount. You know exactly what you are capable of and don't ever let anybody tell you different. The trouble is, the erosion of trust usually begins with you and your abilities. Once this goes, the long slide into loss of self-esteem and confidence begins and before you know it, you're beginning to wonder if you are either paranoid or dreamed it all.

MANNERS

Nothing can beat simple good manners. 'Please' and 'thank you', no matter how small the task, also 'good morning' and 'goodbye'. You may be a stupid fool, but at least the charge of rude, stupid fool will never be levelled at you. Bad manners show that someone has succeeded in annoying you. They may keep pressing on this sensitive spot until they get a more obvious reaction, which will only earn you the label 'oversensitive'. Don't let people know how you might react in any given situation or you will lose the crucial elements of surprise and fear. It's much better to keep them guessing and save your anger for worthwhile occasions when it will be treated with respect.

WHERE TO STAND WHEN THE SHIT IS HITTING THE FAN

Sometimes the best-prepared plans can go horribly wrong. When 'the shit hits the fan' it is obviously advisable to be standing behind one of your colleagues. But since prevention is better than cure, you should make every effort to forestall this unpleasant eventuality. Knowing about the strange and wonderful worlds of paper and words is fundamental to an informed appreciation of the workplace and your rights in it. The most powerful one ordinarily is the world of words, where you are at the mercy of every little thing people say and think, and it is not until a disaster happens that you are propelled like a missile into the other world: the world of paper. Here is to be found your legal protection, the life-preserver you will clutch gratefully to your bosom. At the end of the day people are bound by what is written down. That is why God delivered the Ten Commandments in written form, so that there could be no arguments along the lines of: 'No, he didn't say that. He said: "Thou shalt not covet thy neighbour's *knife*". That's what he said.' 'How to use memos' in Chapter 6 gives you some tips on how to understand and manipulate the world of paper.

five

Identifying alien types

'What do you think the devil's going to look like if he's around?'

TV REPORTER AARON ALTMAN, BROADCAST NEWS

You will meet all sorts of weird and wonderful people in your working life as working unfortunately does not automatically obliterate all aspects of personality. There is every chance you will meet the same kind of loony who approaches you at the bus stop; the difference being that the advanced loony has given up totally the masquerade of normality and is therefore unemployable, whereas the working loony still exhibits some misleading aspects of reasonable behaviour. This section will give you an idea of the kind of people you will meet and where you will meet them.

THE MEN FROM MARS
The New Age Sage

Instantly recognisable by his use of the phrases 'I'm a feminist, you know' and 'Last weekend I got in touch with my inner caveman', his favourite book is Warren Farrell's *The Myth of Male Power* from which he quotes, verbatim. He favours a peculiar form of dress consisting of crumpled linen suits, Italian loafers and a skivvy instead of a tie, like a revved-up version of Phillip Adams. Normally seen in the creative arts or advertising. Wants nothing more in life than to continue to pay off his two-storey terrace (which he is renovating) and to drink fine Australian reds while discussing the dearth of true creativity in the Australian environment.

He will never make a pass at women because firstly, they frighten him and secondly, that would mean too much displaying of ugly emotion, which is his Achilles heel. He will fight to the death to hang on to the power he already has, and in a particularly insidious and vicious form: by exploiting sympathy. He will lull you into a false sense of security, assuring you that he understands your position perfectly, while at the same time telling everybody else that he thinks you may not have the real creativity required for the job. He is so slippery that nobody can get a grip on him.

(The female version of the New Age sage is more sympathetic usually, as she believes it is important to 'be in touch with your feelings'. Her favourite book is *Women Who Run With The Wolves* and she will press this upon you at the earliest opportunity. The more way-out version may even burn aromatic oils at her desk or play tapes with titles like 'Whale Dreaming' or 'Forest Wonderland', which will make you think you accidentally wandered into a camping ground populated solely by New Age-ists.)

Mr Credibility

He will say things like: 'I think a degree is a waste of time. I worked my way up from the bottom. I've put in the hard yards.' He will then tell you about working life in the seventies and how he hung around with anybody who was anybody, then. As you look at the flares and the garish, mismatched tie that he has worn ever since, you realise that 'That was then, this is now' is a phrase he doesn't understand. He has a cache of impressive little stories he trots out on various occasions about the time he said such and such to Richard Neville, and when politics meant something as he recites all the lyrics of 'It's Time' to you. He is essentially harmless unless he is in a position of power in which case he will wreak havoc as he has no proper training or management system and has survived largely on bullshit and mateship. Normally seen in journalism, advertising, public relations or publicity. Anything that requires a large amount of bullshit and a small amount of talent.

He is easy to deflate by simply being better organised than he is. Ask him about the Vietnam protest marches and he'll be your friend for life. Defer to his opinion and ego, write everything down in any verbal meetings (as he is quite capable of changing his mind at a later date and neglecting to tell you) and then do exactly what you want anyway. He'll never know the difference.

(The female version, Ms Credibility, is used to getting what she wants by using the old methods of flirting with senior management, which was fine in the sixties, when she started her career, but doesn't sit so well with some younger colleagues. She has some affectations: designer clothes and calling for 'More Moët!' with gay abandon when celebrating a successful sales pitch.)

The Postwar Depressionist

He grew up during WWII, reached his career peak during the sixties and is nearing the end of his career. Essentially conservative, the Depression still hangs over him like a miasma, as he remembers so clearly the horror stories his parents told him about bread queues. He is not used to women in the workforce in any way, and young, intelligent women shock and threaten him.

His wife has never worked a day in her life and continues to cook his dinner every evening. He brings gladwrapped homemade biscuits and cakes into work, which he eats for morning and afternoon teas. His dress consists of extremely dull suits at the lower end of the spectrum but he has been known to favour body shirts and slacks. The more creative version wears the Safari Suit. He believes in God, The Queen and Nice Evenings Down at the Club. He does not know how to use a computer and still thinks that every female is perfectly qualified to do his typing. He calls you 'dear', very politely.

He can be seen in any industry, but favours education, sales of conservative financial products or medical products like hearing aids or blood pressure machines. Agree with everything he says but bear in mind he disapproves of you anyway, so will use any opportunity to say that you are perhaps 'wilful' and 'inclined to be very creative, but perhaps without the essential attention to detail'. He will shaft you in a very principled fashion. The best way of dealing with him is to have a million good sound reasons for doing what you are doing and be prepared to justify them in a calm and reasonable manner. He is too principled to really have a go at the jugular, but will irritate you on a daily basis.

(The female version of this character is almost non-existent but, when spotted, has been known to favour sensible flat shoes and cardigans.)

The Great Pretender

This man is to be noted for his favourite boast: 'I've been with this company since it started. I helped to build this company from the ground up.' Not only is it sad, it's true. He has an invisible wife, or is divorced. He has spent his whole life working late hours for the company and organising exciting things like sales weekends and company dinners. He believes in the company. He is loyal to it, even more than to himself. He has a misleading, jolly manner but is on the alert for anybody who may threaten or question the company culture. It may be difficult to work out what he actually does, but be assured he is indispensable. You know this because he will tell you so himself, at nine o'clock at night after one too many aspirin. He is to be seen wandering in and out of the MD's office 'organising things'. He is always at the right-hand side of the MD in any company dinner and grovels appealingly to any overseas visitors. He worships the MD and encourages a symbiotic relationship with him. You will be fine as long as you are always extremely polite and don't threaten his relationship with his beloved boss.

(In female form, this character is truly pathetic because it is clear to all and sundry that she doesn't have a life. She has a loud, penetrating voice and an authoritative manner. She refers to all women younger and prettier than herself as 'flakes'. This type can be particularly vicious at after-work drinks when she will tell you several home truths about yourself and speak disparagingly of her ex-husband's sexual prowess while clutching a bottle of gin.)

The Good Bloke

This man is unprincipled: the more so because he appears to be the reverse. He is good mates with everybody and always charming. If not handsome, he is well-groomed, which can pass for good looks. His dress is fashionable but not overtly trendy. He encourages people to talk, while never saying anything about himself. He is the person who always comes up with 'constructive suggestions'. When put on the spot, he will appear to be fair and reasonable. He will support you as long as it is convenient for him. When the time comes for him to withdraw his support he may actually tell you that he is doing this because he is being placed 'in an unenviable position' over which he has no control. He will tell you that he's sure you understand.

He will never make a pass at you or drink too much: he's far too clever for that. He will shaft you dispassionately and mercilessly, believing that if anybody is qualified to have power, it's him. Keep every piece of paper you get from him, make diary notes and do a bit of detective work. He will run over you like a tractor otherwise. He does not necessarily have any talent bar the most important one of smoothing people over. This type appears in every industry, but is particularly insidious in sales or finance. If you can't get anything on him avoid him like the plague.

(For the female version of this character see 'The Corporate Girlie'.)

The Empire Builder

Mediocre, that's what this character is. No creative drive worth mentioning, unless it's in his favourite catchphrase: 'Not better, just bigger!' Assuming, somewhat rightly, that power exists in quantity, not quality, he will gradually expand his division until it bears no resemblance to its original character. With a ballooning ego to bounce him along which expands at roughly the same rate as the department, he is filled with a gratifying sense of responsibility for the number of employees he has. (When he is alone, he will count them.)

Any spare task magically necessitates the creation of a new position, which he must employ somebody to fill. The result is that a strange sense of lethargy coupled with self-importance fills his division: nobody has enough of anything to do. As for the boss himself, he has practically delegated himself out of existence, and spends all his time checking up on people's projects and ordering new desks. He is normally seen in personnel, human resources, banking administration, the public sector and large finance companies.

He will be fine if left to himself, maundering along in his own little corner, but woe betide you if you step on his territory and that includes any minute task that he sees as belonging to his department. He will then drag you through endless meetings trying to say that you either give up the task to him (for which he will employ somebody new, of course) or that you should become part of his department, body and soul. (Oh goodie! That gives him an opportunity to order another desk.) All you can do is tread a fine line between consulting him without coming under his direct control.

(The female version is identical.)

THE WOMEN FROM VENUS
The Control Freak

This woman is dangerous as she is a type all of her own and is not spawned by any particular industry or profession. She can pop up anywhere, usually when you least expect it. She has a life of a sort — a husband very much in the background — but seems to feel that the world owes her something. Since one cannot take on the whole world, she then proceeds to take it out on you. She is paranoid about her reputation and will do anything to ensure that not even a whiff of incompetence or vulnerability ever attaches to her.

To this end she will want to see everything you do, even routine letters. She will edit them and give them back to you and then edit them again when you give them to her to sign. She will say 'yes' to a verbal question as she wants to appear decisive and then will turn around and change her mind as the devil of indecision sits on her shoulder. She does not respond well to verbal agreements but favours little notes written in pen in the margin. They protect her: then there can be no argument about what people may have said: it's all there in black and white.

She is usually quite talented, but nobody ever has time to appreciate it as they are all too busy running for cover. Don't ever take her on over trivialities. Her method of retribution is the same whether it's a triviality or not. Who wants to get bitten in the neck every day? Save your fire for something really important: your professional reputation. Then use everything you have. Until then, all you can do is submit graciously and hope that she gets run over by the number 342 bus and has to spend a few months in hospital.

(The male version is almost identical but is inclined to be slightly less paranoid about incompetence. He uses the frown and the bulging eyes to keep people in line to the point where they wouldn't dare make a mistake.)

The Boss's Wife

Since time out of mind, this type has been causing trouble. She's still there, thick on the ground, and is only now beginning to be challenged by her opposite: The Boss's Husband.

Usually seen in small to middling businesses in hospitality or manufacturing, this woman is under the mistaken impression that she actually started the company, when in fact it was her husband. But to her, she is her husband, so it boils down to the same thing. If you are a woman, she will probably hate you instantly. If you are a man, she will flirt with you. She has made a lifestyle of being accommodating: if her husband favours very fashionable clothes she will too, if he wears old jeans and a windy, she will too. But however she looks she has an unmistakable air of being 'looked after'.

She will engage you in a spurious attempt to be your work colleague but don't fall for it for a second. When he's not there, she is the boss. She is a self-styled spy and can do more damage to you than a straight-out discussion with your boss can. She can make sure you get the sack, by insinuation. Never go to her house for dinner and never tell her anything about your personal life. If it isn't going well, this will be attributed to a fault of character on your part, which, in turn, will call your competence into question. If she likes you, all you can do is be extremely polite to her; if she doesn't, you're not going to last long anyway.

Daddy's Little Girl

This woman has not yet grasped the fact that she is not at home. At home, she has been used to sobbing, pleading or throwing tantrums to get her own way; at work she behaves in exactly the same fashion. She maintains a pleasant fiction that, at home, her family adores her. You suspect that what she attributes to adoration is actually acquiescence. They've just been worn down by constant tantrums and sulking, like a mother having her skirt pulled persistently by a child. She has some talent, but relies on one emotion to get her through: pity. She is always whining about something or other: the fact that her chilblains have come back, that her acne is getting worse, that her poor salary means that she has to work weekends, that her sister-in-law was really horrible to her at the last family funeral. Because she is not usually very attractive, you feel even more sorry for her. Her workstation drips with mementos of the holiday in Bali, or photographs of her sister's wedding, or her cute niece/nephew, even pictures of Tom Cruise and George Clooney.

She is infantile: when she wants something she will beg and plead ('Please, Dad, please'), when she wants to get at somebody she will create a situation of unfairness ('Mum, Daniel just hit me!'). She is a slavering, sobbing, pathetic example of attention-getting. Her boss, usually a man, feels sorry for her and she places him in the unenviable position of father/protector. Women, however, know better. If you are a woman and her boss, she'll be a bit worried: you know all the games and actually expect her to work.

Thus begins the gradual assassination of your character and its virtues. When you reprimand her, she will go running to the nearest man to say how 'unfair' and 'horrible' you are, in her baby-doll voice. To prevent being seen as the big meanie in the whole affair, anything you have to say to her should be said in the safety of the office car park or the pub. A veiled, or not so veiled, threat will usually do the trick. If she tells anybody, deny it. After that, play her little game of character assassination: play on the hypochondria, the tendency to neuroticism and finish off with the unchallengable sentence: 'Of course, there is a strong streak of madness in her family, poor thing, so what can you expect?'

(There is no known male equivalent of Daddy's Little Girl, unless it is the man who still lives with his mother. He is in awe of women and giggles nervously whenever one approaches. He is too neurotic to be a threat in any way at all.)

The Obstacle Maker

This woman should really be working for the municipal council, so skilled is she at diversion. She is a unique combination of the Control Freak and the Empire Builder. She favours clothes which make her blend into the background: brown is a favourite colour. High heels are out: they impede progress as she chases people waving bits of paper. She feels that, somewhere along the line, somebody took something away from her without asking. Now, she has been given the God-sent opportunity to say 'no' to everybody else, which she does on a depressingly regular basis. The only reason she says 'no' is because she can. In some rare situations her 'no' might save your reputation: but rest assured, that wouldn't have been her intention.

She is normally seen in the financial industry, accounting, administration or the public sector, anywhere where she can use official forms and sanctions to make her 'no' more resonant and powerful. She loves triplicate copies, red pens and her filing cabinet. She is always saying 'You can't do that because'... To quash ideas or innovations is her mission in life. She loathes imagination: possessing none herself, she is frightened by it. One cannot put imagination on a form. Therefore, she will make you fill out three forms, which have to be signed by six different people (usually not in their office) before something as routine as sending a courier can be achieved. This kind of person usually does the pay as well, so it is wise to remain on her good side. She is an immovable object, and it is up to you to work out ways of getting round her. Do this by asking her about her life: she appears so dull that everybody assumes she doesn't have one. Charm her into submission — flatter her, flirt with her. Make the ultimate sacrifice and have lunch with her. Soon, you will be able to get her to do things in half the time, and perhaps ignore some of the restraints altogether.

(The male equivalent is identical.)

The Corporate Girlie

Yep, she's got it all. She's got two degrees, the power suit, the walk, the attitude. She's on the fast track and you'd better not stand between her and her future unless you want to be a mere flattened ribbon complete with tyre marks. She's cool, competent and she's got what it takes. She knows all the rules — that is why you will never see her carrying a copy of this book.

She is the New Breed but still knows enough to be grateful to her older sisters who paved the way for her. She is careful about when she calls herself a 'feminist', saying she is to older women and saying she isn't to younger ones. Sometimes she'll wear the suit, at other times she'll come in wearing her Doc Martens and paisley shirt, just so that you realise she still knows the meaning of 'cutting edge'. She will have drinks with the boys, but will never get plastered, and is certainly never caught out in an indiscretion. She is everything to everybody. Her style and competence means that she is nearly at the top of the tree, but is bashing her head against the glass ceiling of the sky as her youth and talent count against her.

As she's so close to the top, she's very jealous of her achievements and will view you with a sort of friendly suspicion. It is probably wise to become her friend: a sister or brother in adversity. Be frank with her and imply that you know how hard it is being the only woman in management. If you are a woman, make sure you consult her opinion and go to her with any male-related power problems in the office. After all, a friend at the top can never hurt. On her own she'll be fair while protecting her territory, but pray that she will never get together with The Good Bloke.

The Two-Faced Bitch

This is the situation: you're at a party, you walked through the door five seconds ago, and already a person has backed you up against the wall and is behaving like your best friend.

You are amazed. You think 'Wow! A genuine soul. Somebody who can see past all the garbage and can see that I am a really cool, intelligent person!' After you come back from the bathroom, looking forward to continuing this really quite stimulating conversation, the person says to you: 'Look I'm sorry. I made a bit of a mistake. I thought you were somebody.' And you're left sitting there like a gasping fish on a boulder.

So it is with this woman. She will come up to you on your first or second day in the company and tell you things. Things about other people. Not very nice things, but it's all done under the guise of being 'helpful'. She is immensely dissatisfied in her job, being more intelligent than the job she is employed to do, but not skilled or talented enough to hold a position of more power. She has a nice wide smile and looks innocuous enough (you'll think to yourself 'She's a nice girl') but she is deadly. She will be nice to you until she realises she can't get anything from you, then she will treat you like a refugee from a leper colony. In fact, your jaw will drop and your eyes will bulge at the blatant and audacious way she will do this, so that she will make you think you actually may be a leper.

She's a blatant mix of Daddy's Little Girl and a hissing viper. She will stab you in the back on any occasion and look wide-eyed at anybody who accuses her of unprofessional behaviour. The best thing you can do is treat her exactly the same as everybody else. Never go to lunch with her, never be seen in a one-on-one conversation with her. Don't tell her about your mistakes, only your successes. Look for an opportunity to set her up big-time — given the chance she'll do exactly the same to you.

Things you should know about work that nobody ever told you

six

'A woman loses 50 per cent of her authority when people find out who she's sleeping with.' *CORPORATE SUPERBITCH BRIDGET GREGORY,* THE LAST SEDUCTION

PERCEPTION IS REALITY

It is in this area where your personality and character can be set in stone for the rest of the time you are with the company. It doesn't matter that you work loyally, faithfully, competently at your job if *nobody sees you doing it.* So you have to institute a public relations campaign for yourself. This is easy in service-oriented jobs, where visibility is everything, less easy in vague, officey jobs. If you obey the Rules of Success, you will have a better chance of the perception being in your favour. Perception comes from the people with the power: your MD, your direct supervisor and the person they listen to, who could be the boss's assistant or the manager of the accounting department. It could be, in fact, just about anybody, but if you've done your schmoozing, you should know who that person is.

The perception could be that you are 'difficult', a 'troublemaker', or a 'bitch'. Never mind that you aren't a bitch and only told the receptionist to 'Shut up, for God's sake you stupid woman!' because this was the fiftieth time she'd told you the story of her grasping, selfish sister who 'took the rings off his hands before the body had even cooled, I tell you'; the perception will be that you *are* a bitch.

The perception might be that you have a fairly slack attitude toward your job because you turn up at 9.30 most mornings. It doesn't matter if you work until 7.00 every night if everybody who matters left at 5.30 pm. For all they know, you probably left at 5.31 pm — it's that bad attitude of yours.

AVOIDING BECOMING THE PHANTOM — BEING VISIBLE

Perception and visibility operate in tandem. The best way of avoiding a perception problem is to be visible and adopt a PR campaign. Use the Brownie Points Accumulator on pages 72–73 to ascertain the number of points you will get for each positive PR activity. The aim is to accumulate eight to ten points per month.

True Crimes — Real Life Story

Nicola had a perception problem. She never seemed to be in her office.

The company had recently moved premises and, as light came in from only one side of the building, had built the new offices from glass partitioning. Nicola's most recent job (as an administrative assistant) required her to process all the company monies and to handle routine paper matters.

'I had just about the worst position in the whole place,' she says. 'I had the very first office in the row. Everybody had to walk past my office to get to theirs, including the managing director. It was the habit of every person to look into that office as they came in. My job meant I was often away from my desk discussing matters of procedure with people. I think I saw the MD walk past my office once in the whole year I was there, which meant he saw me about the same.

'All it took,' continues Nicola in a depressed tone, 'was for me to make a couple of mistakes and suddenly I had the tag of "slacker". The MD never saw me, you see. All he ever saw was an empty office. Soon they were monitoring me, I became nervous, and before I knew it, I'd lost the job.'

This sad little tale illustrates clearly the maxim 'perception is reality' and the old chestnut that people who live in glass offices should make a bit of an effort to stay in them.

IDENTIFYING CORPORATE MYTHS
Work is a democracy

We may live in a so-called democracy, but don't imagine that work is anything like one; if it could be likened to any system of government it would be that known as benevolent dictatorship. The French King Louis XIV's form of government was dignified by this term: all it meant was that he built a spectacularly beautiful palace, Versailles, and treated the serfs a bit better than they were used to. Your employers may try and make you believe that everything is fair and equal but don't ever believe them: it isn't true.

Work is extremely hierarchical. At the top is the MD (the monarch) followed by senior management (nobles), middle management (landed gentry) and everybody else (serfs). Firstly, it doesn't matter how fair and just you are:

THE BROWNIE POINTS ACCUMULATOR

No. of points

☿ Turn up on time and say 'goodnight' to everybody.

1 point per month

☿ Always say a couple of positive things about a project you intend to sink.

1 point per project

☿ When you do something spectacular or worthy, write a diffident memo about it and copy it to all management for either their comments or 'FYI' (for your information).

1 point per five memos

☿ If a client comments in an admiring fashion on your work, ask them (tactfully) to put it in writing and send it to your boss. Every little bit helps when accumulating Brownie points.

1 point per written letter

☿ Be seen having lunch at your desk at least once a week.

1 point per month

☿ Wander past the boss's open door and stick your head in with a routine query at least once a day.

1 point per month

☿ If you see an interesting article that relates to your industry, photocopy it and circulate it to management — if you haven't done anything spectacular for a while, it will keep you in people's minds and will show that you maintain a healthy interest in your industry.

5 points per month

☿ Mask a chat by a work-related question (make an effort to appear interested) with the people who have the real power every couple of days: this will keep you in touch with what's really going on.

3 points per month

☿ Always say 'What an interesting idea!' and 'Good on you!'

1 point per month

☿ If you've worked on a project jointly, always give part of the credit to the other party and acknowledge their good ideas. The person involved will appreciate this — everybody likes good PR — and will probably do the same for you.

2 points per project

☿ Always think of ways of increasing business, saving money or increasing productivity — come up with a ripper of an idea at least once a quarter. MDs love that stuff.

3 points per project

☿ Better yet, be even smarter and come up with an idea, discuss it with your immediate superior and make them think it's a joint effort, showering glory on all involved.

5 points per project

☿ Bring something in to work — lamingtons are a good choice — everybody will see you as you offer them around and will think you're a very nice person to do something so thoughtful, particularly if you allow them to think you actually baked them yourself.

2 points per baking

☿ Work late every fortnight — late enough to leave either at the same time, or just after, the MD.

2 points per month

☿ Ask the opinon or advice of at least one influential person per month.

2 points per month per person

what matters at the end of the day is what you achieved. Managers are not interested in pathetic excuses, they only want to know whether you did the job they directed. They don't care if people stood in your path, or projects were blocked. ('I don't care that you spent most of the second quarter besieged inside the castle. So what if you fell in the moat and nearly drowned? That's your problem.') Secondly, have you contributed in a positive way to the company? By this they mean initiating things. ('So, did you think up a new way of taxing the pig-pens?') Thirdly, do you get on with your colleagues or do they think you have an attitude problem? ('The Honourable Sir de Cimate tells me that you did not rape and pillage with alacrity and enjoyment when you sacked his enemy's castle. Is this true?') This last is the most important and can be a good reason to start initiating the sacking process, on the pretext of your doubtful competence. ('I'm afraid it's the thumbscrew and rack for you, my friend. Just follow me down into this dank cavern.')

Quite often, you will see people treated with favouritism. For some reason, the boss really likes them and they are promoted over people who are far more competent. Some people seem to be able to make heaps of mistakes and get away with them. Some people are just born lucky. This is just the way life is and unless you are one of these exceptional or lucky people, the best you can do is to read this book and start polishing the rough and grating edges off your personality.

They're running the place, they must be intelligent

Whoa! Not necessarily. With some MDs you may think 'How the hell did they get where they got?' There are usually a number of reasons: they have mates in high places; they're related to somebody in high places; they're totally unscrupulous; they're corrupt; they're lucky; or the people in high places haven't latched onto them yet. If you're working with incompetent management (see 'The poisoned chalice') you're not going to make much progress until they're given the boot.

They're in menial positions, they must be dumb
Also, not necessarily so. Sometimes you may think 'Why are they doing this job? They're so smart.' It's usually for one of two reasons: they have no ambition or they're being blocked, and consequently they want to move but they can't.

It's not personal
This is absolute rubbish as every decision made is extremely personal. Luckily for business, and at its most positive and effective, the decision which is made for 'sound business reasons' sometimes coincides with the professional strengths of the person involved, as in 'We'll give Darren that difficult client, as he is very good at smoothing people over'. You may excel at some things, and not be as good at others; therefore, one hopes, you will be given tasks at which you excel, and the other tasks will be given to somebody else. At the most negative end of the spectrum, you may have a perceived 'attitude problem' in which case it becomes extremely personal. They want you out and they will do anything it takes to achieve this. It's up to you to work out which one it is.

UNDERSTANDING THE PETER PRINCIPLE
In a nutshell, this principle asserts that everybody will rise to the level of their own incompetence. By appreciating this, you will understand why your boss is such a fool. At the exact point when competence becomes incompetence, because the person has neither the skills nor the

intelligence to meet the demands of the new, more responsible position, the Peter Principle is cogently demonstrated. They couldn't help themselves — ego and ambition drove them to it.

SEX AND GOSSIP

These are both very tempting and hard to resist, but don't do either (and certainly not both together). Listen to gossip, if you must, but don't be an active participant. Practically all the information will be useless. Real, useful information will be given to you by one person, seriously and confidentially. It's the same with sex. If you do find you harbour feelings of lust and lunchtime fantasies toward one of your work colleagues, have a cup of tea and read Linda Jaivin's *Eat Me* instead. That'll put you off.

WORK FUNCTIONS AND SOCIAL FUNCTIONS

The former you have to attend, the latter you don't. The difference is that the company pays for one and you pay for the others. Work functions are sales dinners, annual dinners and dinners with your boss. Social functions are with your work colleagues and can constitute anything from drinks after work, to barbeques on the weekend. Don't go to these. They are extremely dull. All anybody talks about is work and it encourages dangerous, flirtatious behaviour. Besides, do you really want people to think you don't have a life?

AVOIDING THE TAG OF VILLAGE IDIOT — WHAT TO SAY WHEN YOU'RE STUCK IN THE LIFT WITH THE MD

Although instant petrification is usually the result of this, what about saying 'Hello' or 'Good morning'? If they say 'Who are *you*?' put a paper bag over your head and forget about it. You have only a short time, but in that time you should try and say something intelligent. The weather is safe, but boring. If they have a sense of humour, you could try a joke but make sure it's nothing crass or anything that involves dead babies or animals. A sure-fire winner is 'I like your tie/blouse'. This is their cue to tell you the story of the buying or receiving of this item of clothing.

THE WINDOW OF OPPORTUNITY

This is the period of time between a mistake being made and when people discover it has been made. It could be any amount of time at all: from 15 minutes to a couple of days or weeks. This is crucial time: while the Window of Opportunity is still open, you must work out what you are going to do to recover from this mistake so that the least amount of damage is traced back to you. After the window has closed, there's no point in trying to change anybody's perception of why the mistake was made and who was, ultimately, responsible for it. It's like running after a train as it's leaving the platform. Pointless.

THE CLAYTON'S DEADLINE

It's a good idea when you have deadlines, to make up your own deadline of a week or two before the real deadline. With any project that you are dealing with any number of things can go wrong at any time, particularly if you are relying on other people. The Clayton's Deadline will help you to minimise the risk — if you're working to this, then you've given yourself a Window of Opportunity to use in case something goes wrong.

WHEN TO TELL A LITTLE WHITE LIE

You don't have to be scrupulously honest all the time. If the real world operated like that we'd all be dead or not speaking to one another. A lie is very useful during the Window of Opportunity. 'My computer has crashed' is a handy stand-by when a project is due and you haven't done it. Of course, your computer would be working if you hadn't unplugged a bit of it. 'I never received that memo' can be used when you have seen it and haven't done it. If they say 'But you should have' continue to deny it and do so until the subject is dropped.

Never tell the truth if people ask you what you think of their haircut, especially if it looks like somebody put a bowl on their head and cut around it. When somebody says 'I'm fat' or 'I'm stupid' always say 'Don't be ridiculous'. When somebody says 'What do you think of this idea?' always say 'It's a very interesting idea', no matter what you think of it.

GETTING THROUGH YAWNO MEETINGS

Meetings can be a minefield of potential successes or disasters. Because of their rambling nature, meetings provide a perfect opportunity for people to criticise or praise you. A lot of damage to your reputation can be done in an apparently innocuous meeting. If there are more than three people in a meeting, you can be guaranteed that no decisions will be made and it will go on forever. You know it's going to be very long when the boss says 'Should we have some lunch brought in?' At this juncture, it would be wise to go for a walk around the block under the guise of going to the bathroom.

Meetings usually follow a certain procedure:

The agenda

Most organised companies have an agenda. This constitutes what you are going to discuss, which means that you are expected to prepare for it. Look at every item carefully and work out if you are supposed to contribute to any of them. If you haven't done some of the things, do them as soon as possible, invent a plausible reason why you haven't done them, or set a date for doing them. What is important is that you show you made some progress on this project since the last meeting. If you really haven't done anything at all you can use another colleague as a good excuse, as in 'We're having a meeting on that tomorrow', and follow it up with a quick diversionary tactic, as in 'Which reminds me, what did happen to that report which said our product causes cancer?'

Disorganised companies don't have agendas. Points are raised at will, discussion is all over the place and the meeting goes on for a couple of days. These are the worst of all, because they practically invite horror questions from left field. These are backstabbing goes at you disguised as innocent questions. They usually focus on insignificant detail or 'what if' situations. These are questions such as: 'How many people did you sample in this survey and what criteria did you use?'; 'By the way, what is the name of the business editor of *Wagga Wagga Land Review*?'; or 'Have you thought about what you will do if the client goes to the toilet and refuses to come out?' Prepare for anything and watch for attacks.

The discussion

This is the soporific section of the meeting, in which it will be all that you can manage to do to keep your eyes open. If it's not your project, make one constructive comment or ask one question and then lapse into a stupor. If it's your project you will have to stay awake, unfortunately. You should know your stuff. Write up a list of questions you might be asked and prepare your answers. If a left-fielder comes in your direction, counter it with a flattering question such as 'What action would you recommend?', or 'I wasn't quite sure how to manage that. Has anybody got any suggestions?' (This is a good one, as everybody will have to bestir themselves.) If that fails, create a diversion.

Always bring in a pad and make notes on it during the discussion. Whatever you do, don't doodle. I was once hauled up in a performance review for doodling as they considered it to be evidence of a 'lack of interest in the proceedings'. Of course, I wasn't interested — at least, not interested enough to take notes — but I was listening. To management, interest means note-taking.

Take in everything you will need during the meeting — all the relevant bits of paper, files and research texts (the larger the better). Having lots of stuff looks like you know what you're doing and means that you don't have to keep running out to get things, which makes you look like you're disorganised.

Other matters

Here we come to the most ominous part of the meeting. It's the item right at the end and consists of all the things that nobody could think of when the agenda was being written or anything that has come up during the meeting. This section provides a field day for boomerangs that you accidentally set in motion. Think over the Worst Case Scenario (all the things you haven't done), the Best Case Scenario (all the things you've done), prepare for both and think on your feet.

During this discussion smile and look interested. Never cross your arms. If somebody starts on at you, use the retorts listed in earlier passages. Always say something positive about somebody's idea. Try not to yawn openly. (There is a method of yawning with your mouth shut which is not visible to anybody else. All that happens is a slight elongation of the nostrils. Practise this in front of the mirror at home.)

Sometimes meetings can degenerate into bunfights if the MD either isn't there or encourages this kind of behaviour. I have been in meetings where people have been reduced to saying 'What would you know? You're goddamn stupid!' I was in a meeting once where somebody threw a half-eaten asparagus roll at somebody else. Needless to say, this kind of behaviour is not acceptable. Keep yourself above the fray. Always be calm and maintain a professional manner.

If you're really under fire you can do one of two things: pause, say calmly 'I really do have to go the bathroom', get up and think up something while you're in there, or say 'I wasn't prepared for this question as it wasn't on the agenda. Can I get back to you this afternoon/tomorrow/next week?' This is perfectly legitimate. (The former we do not recommend except in situations of extremity. Leaving the room when you're under fire will give people the opportunity to say anything they want about you, and by the time you get back to the meeting you discover that decisions have been made in your absence and you've been given a new job, like cleaning out the rubbish bins.)

If somebody is making personal remarks say calmly, while smiling, 'I really do object to your tone. I'd like to keep this discussion on a professional level.' This is tantamount to a declaration of war in work parlance. If the situation is at the level of throwing asparagus rolls, then get up, gather up your stuff and say 'I think we should continue this meeting when everybody has calmed down' and leave the room.

Minutes

Minutes are usually taken as a record of what occurred in the meeting and what decisions were made. Always read the minutes carefully to check that you haven't been given something to do of which you have no recollection. (Before you make a fuss, double-check that it really wasn't discussed — you don't want to be caught not paying attention.) In important meetings — performance reviews, for example — you may be required to sign the minutes. Never sign anything unless you understand it and agree with it and don't let people bully or hurry you. You are entitled to ask that any comments you made at the meeting that are not included be included. You are also entitled to add your own comments on a separate sheet of paper before you sign the final copy. If the minutes are used later to justify a bad performance or sacking, you'll want to have your comments noted.

TRANSLATING THE LANGUAGE — AN INTRODUCTION TO WORKSPEAK

You'd better keep your alien translator with you at all times, because you are entering the zone of Workspeak. It is not unlike the Newspeak to be found in George Orwell's *1984,* which was designed to limit the imagination and control the populace. Workspeak seeks to do this by giving managers lots of opportunities to protect their backs, deflect criticism, camouflage devious plans and confuse their underlings.

Although there are no classes in Workspeak, and it is not a language that is studied or even considered outside the work environment, everybody who is successful at work knows its meaning and knows how to use it. (It is commonly thought it is learned by osmosis.)

Workspeak is ephemeral and amazingly flexible. It enables you to say one thing while meaning another. It provides you with a tool for attack while appearing polite. It enables you to cover up your true intentions and thoughts with politically correct, acceptable phrases.

There are some key phrases and words you should learn to become an expert practitioner of Workspeak. (See the section 'Phrases that will get you out of trouble', and the glossary of terms at the back of this book.)

But first, here's an example of how Workspeak works. We'll run through an imaginary job interview with two people, one answering in plain English, the other in Workspeak.

'So, you were sacked from your last job?'
Plain English: 'Yep. Thank God! Bunch of jerks.'
Workspeak: 'I felt that I had achieved all I could. It was a mutually gratifying parting.'

'You've had a few jobs in your time. Why is that?'
Plain English: 'I get bored very easily.'
Workspeak: 'Not only do I contribute all I have learned to the company, but I try and learn as much as I can as well. When the position no longer holds a challenge for me and I can't contribute on the level that I'm used to, I look for new opportunities.'

'Oh, you've worked for Acme. I used to work there. Did you know Steve Jones [a renowned Great Pretender]? How did you find working with him?'
Plain English: 'Hated him. A buffoon. A fool!'
Workspeak: 'Steve was an interesting person. But there's always some difficulties when a person gets enthusiastic about so many projects at the same time.'

'Why do you want to work for our company?'
Plain English: 'Well, I need the money. And I like what you do.'
Workspeak: 'I find the work you do here very exciting. I feel my skills can be used and appreciated properly here. It would be a great challenge.'

'What do you think of the design for this new product we're working on?'
Plain English: 'I don't think much of it.'

Workspeak: 'I liked the overall design and the colour of the typeface. However, I feel that the artist has not really grasped the overall concept. Perhaps they could come up with a few more designs?'

Do you see how it works? It's like a bottle of sugar-coated pills. There are variations on Workspeak. We're all familiar with Polispeak, and Entertainspeak is used by celebrities around the world. When confronted with the question 'What do you think of our country?' when all they've seen is the airport tarmac and the front door of their hotel, they never say: 'How would I know? I've been here five minutes' or 'Yuck! I'd rather be at home by the pool'; they always say: 'Oh, it's lovely. Beautiful. I'd love to live here if my work permitted.'

Although there are some excellent practitioners of Workspeak in the private sector, particularly at the senior management level, the real maestros are the bureaucrats in federal government, who have managed to turn Workspeak into an art form.

ASKING QUESTIONS

Communication is one of the major keys to success at work. Ask as many questions as you can about everything, in as tactful a manner as possible. Firstly, simple things that have been shrouded previously in a dark cloud of mystery, that everybody else takes for granted, will be revealed to you. Secondly, you would be surprised at the number of things people do that appear to have no rhyme or reason. In fact, a lot of the time, they are doing things simply because they've always been done or done that way. Thirdly, what appears to be an amazingly stupid or simple question may be the best one of all to ask, as it can serve to clarify the situation.

Asking questions (using Workspeak) is a wonderful tool to use when dealing with difficult bosses. If you don't know why you are doing what you are doing then you're going to stuff up somewhere along the line. The key is to bounce the question back to them like a laser beam to either make them clarify the situation or give you some idea of their expectations. Here are some examples of some useful questions to ask when:

Your boss is a Control Freak and nothing you do is ever good enough:
'I'll just run through it again — is this what you're looking for?'
'Is there anything I should pay special attention to when doing this project?'

Your boss is blaming you for a mistake he/she made:
'Did I make a mistake in sending out that purchase order as you directed?'
'Is it true that the MD is blaming me for the failure of our sales campaign?'

Your boss fills you with fear and trembling:
'What can we both do to improve the situation and make both our jobs more rewarding?'

You want to delegate a task to somebody else:
'Will you support my turning over the photocopying and distribution of the sales figures to Robert?'

You have a better idea to increase profits than your boss does:
'If I can show that we can achieve bigger profits or better service with a different approach (that is, a better idea than yours) will you support it?'

Your boss refers to you as 'This Idiot' in a room full of clients:
'Are you aware of how embarrassed I was by your comment this morning?'

You're working with someone who finds tying their shoelaces a task filled with difficulty:
'Is the task/job creating as much strain for you as it appears?'
'Are you finding this job as satisfying as you expected?'

You're living in a communication vacuum — you have no idea if they like what you are doing or if they even notice you are there:
'If I fill out a performance review form, will you have a look at it for me?'

You speak, but it is as if you are talking into a void:
'A fortnight ago I gave you a memo. Do you have any comments on it?'

Your boss wants you to tell the client that his product is rubbish:
'Wouldn't it be better for the client to hear it from the most senior person available?'
'Can you explain to me why it would be a good idea for *me* to do this?'

ANSWERING QUESTIONS

Lots and lots of people have been caught out by the way they answer questions. Asking a question at work is the journalistic equivalent of getting somebody drunk and then quoting every ill-advised thing they say. From your point of view, not answering the question is the Australian equivalent to the American habit of 'taking the fifth' (their Fifth Amendment, commonly used during the McCarthy era: 'I refuse to answer that question on the grounds that it may incriminate me').

Questions such as 'How old are you?' and 'What are your feelings on group sex?' can be answered in any way you prefer. More ominous questions are: 'What do you think of Amanda?' and 'What is your company turnover?' The first can easily be taken care of by saying 'She seems to know what she's doing', while the latter presents difficulties. Nobody asks questions like this without a reason. If you're speaking to the person face-to-face you can say nothing and smile. It requires an unflinching gaze to carry off, but is off-putting for the interviewer and makes them feel foolish. If you can't manage this (and you have to have a lot of attitude to do it successfully) you can try the joke, as in 'Oh, about $2.50, I think' or answer with a question, as in 'What do you want to know for?' or a succinct 'Why?'. It's always best if you can find out why they want to know what they want to know. Then you can determine if they need to know. Always remember: *engage brain before speaking*.

HOW TO USE MEMOS

Memos (memorandums) are a great way of using Workspeak in written form. Anything on paper is always more valuable than anything anybody says, which is why you should be careful about what you write and how you write it. The memo is a way of pointing the finger if something goes wrong. (As you will notice, in the work environment your stuff-ups are all your own, whereas successes are usually the result of 'a great team effort'.)

If you're not sure about something, then bounce it off somebody verbally first. Then later, if things stuff up, you can always say there was a 'communication' problem.

You can tell a project is taken seriously when there are memos about it. This means that there is no doubt about who is taking responsibility if it goes wrong and gives everybody the opportunity to jump on the bandwagon of success.

There are three kinds of memos: the information memo, the protection memo and the warning memo. You can combine the information memo with the protection memo, but the warning memo usually stands alone. It's a good idea to perfect your memo writing at an early stage, then you can use this tool at any time you may need it. Always read all memos — people often bury important information in them and nothing from the outside world could possibly be as important as something from inside the organisation.

The information memo

This consists of pretty standard stuff like notification of meetings or questions that you need answered by senior management that have to be on paper. Remember to send copies to everybody who should be going to the meeting, and anybody who may have to enter details of the meeting in somebody's diary.

The protection memo

This can be used as a way of stating that the project is proceeding or to flag potential problems which if not addressed could lead to some degree of blame attaching to yourself.

Imagine you are working for a large mining company which is about to start digging in a politically sensitive area. There are several large growth areas which will have to be dug up to achieve this. It's not rainforest, just bushland, but you know the greenies will take this as an opportunity to show how, once again, big business is destroying the world. To show that the company cares about what the public thinks, it is holding a series of public forums to discuss the issue. This is really a blind: the decision has already been made, but they want people to think their opinion matters and they don't want any adverse media attention — it all has to be done at a submerged level.

This is the kind of memo you should write in this situation:

MEMORANDUM

To: Your Boss
From: You
CC: The MD, all senior management, anybody else working on project
Re: Public forums on new mining project

A few issues of sensitivity have been raised regarding the projected public forums. Are there any established areas of policy or direction we can follow to ensure that the company achieves its objectives in the following situations:

1. The media
What is company policy regarding this? As the forums are advertised as 'public forums' it may be unwise to deny access to the media, leading to assertions of secretiveness on our part. If we decide not to allow media access, what direction would the company like to take if they arrive and insist on admission?

2. Invitations to environmentalists
Environmentalists may be able to assert that we did not canvass a wide range of opinion for our forum if they are not invited. They may also alert sympathetic media to the forums themselves. What is company policy on this issue?

3. Refreshments
Should they be served at this event or not? If so, should alcohol be served or just tea and coffee? What are your recommendations?

I look forward to your comments and recommendations at the earliest possible opportunity to ensure the success of our public forums.

In this memo, you have done two things: you have protected yourself as well as involving others in any possible disaster.

The warning memo
The doyen of all memos, it is unmistakable. It is usually sent from your boss to you and constitutes a warning sign that all is not well. The warning memo looks something like this:

MEMORANDUM

To: You
From: Your Boss
CC: His/her Boss and possibly personnel
Re: Various matters

New packaging for Spink Ink bottle
It has come to my attention, through the art department, that you have briefed them three times on this packaging idea. This is, quite frankly, a ridiculous waste of time. This project is already running late and we don't need more time wasted. I will talk to you about this when I return from interstate.

Copy for brochure
Where is this? We discussed this weeks ago, and I still haven't seen the final copy. To be discussed on my return.

Computer statistics on last three product launches
Where are these? They are supposed to be with finance before the end of the quarter.

Your travel interstate
You will now not be going interstate to brief our major client. Until these issues are sorted out, all plans are on hold.

If you ever get one of these, you are in big trouble and will have to spend a lot of useful time fixing the situation. Drop all projects (except the super-urgent ones) and spend your time on this matter. The problem seems to be lack of communication. You've mentioned these issues to your boss, but may not have clarified their consequences, and since then much of the content of these verbal exchanges has been forgotten. If there's a misconception, correct it. If you've taken action, but neglected to tell your boss, tell him or her now, verbally and on paper.

What happened with the ink bottle was that somebody from the art department had a whinge, exaggerating the situation. Go and discuss the issue with that person. Then explain to you boss that you have *two* deadlines: *your* deadline and *the* deadline, and that only the former is late. Now is the time to prove how organised you are by showing that you have built in contingency time. Acknowledge your boss's concerns, but emphasise the importance of correct packaging to the success of the project.

Copy for brochure: You've done this. It's still sitting under a pile of papers on his desk. He's forgotten about it. Point this out by saying, as nicely as possible, that you know he's really busy, which explains it.

Computer statistics: Correct. The end of the month went past three days ago, but you've spoken to finance: they're annoyed but they can wait.

Travel interstate: This is designed as a punishment. Don't even bother bringing it up.

Keep all memos that are warning memos or protection memos. Keep them at home. We wouldn't want a mysterious fire to start at work and destroy all our records now, would we?

VISIONS, VALUES AND OTHER CORPORATE FAIRYTALES — SURVIVING CORPORATE TRAINING TECHNIQUES

Most companies have what is known as a training program. This is another form of induction into an alien environment. These are usually extremely silly, and require a level of participation that would defy the belief of an eight-year-old. It doesn't matter if you believe it or not; what matters is that you defer and pay lip-service to it (Workspeak is very useful for this).

In the long run, training programs are unnecessary for people with reasonable skills for the job: that is, a pulse. Those of us who are going cold, however, need these programs as we need the boundary on a football field: it is the company's way of saying 'don't run past these lines or bad things will happen to you'.

The grand vision

During your first induction, somebody will give you a convincing impression of Julius Caesar looking across the ocean, contemplating the invasion of barbarian Britain. This is the Grand Vision Act and will be accompanied by an impassioned speech concerning the company's future. 'I see this company's greatest asset as its people,' this person will say to you. 'We understand people, and that's why service is our greatest selling point. In the years to come, this company will be setting a standard of service that will be renowned around the world' and then the speaker will sigh while looking in a distant and clairvoyant manner at his/her cherished view of the harbour.

In some ways, this is a good thing, as it means that these people may have a fair idea where they are going and are not meandering all over the place, like a drunk who, when walking, makes full use of the pavement and the gutter as well. But in reality, the vision statement is really irrelevant to your day-to-day life. It is only useful in two particular situations: when you're in a sticky situation and you can quote it back to somebody to justify something that you did, or as a way of amassing Brownie points with senior management. You do this by picking up key words and phrases from the vision statement and throwing them back, either verbally or in written form, when you're doing a big project. This will show them that you are a team player and understand and value the future of the company.

The induction process

During this process, you will be told a pack of nonsense about how fair and wonderful the company is and how, if you stick with them, your career will be assured. Don't believe a word of it, it's all rubbish. This is not the way they are, but the way they would like to be. Just smile and nod and ask a question or two. Some large companies have long induction processes in which you pick up some useful information (like how to use the computer) as well as a whole pile of useless words. It is a mild form of brainwashing and should be ignored.

The psychological test

These are utter nonsense. Some written tests supposedly determine your personality and therefore the kind of job that you would be best at, but I know of a man who was a white-collar criminal and in the last personality test he did, the results were that he was sincere, honest, trustworthy and kind to animals, all of which I knew from experience to be totally untrue.

I also knew a woman who, after months of very expensive tests, was told that she was judicious, careful and attentive to detail. Her husband said: 'If they had rung me up, they could have found that out in five minutes. It's the same way she does the dishes.' The only thing tests like these really determine is that you can successfully do a test.

If you do one of these silly tests and the results say that you would make a good administrator and you have spent your entire career buried under a mountain of paper, then you might want to make an appointment for a verbal interview as well, where you say that, perhaps, administration is not your greatest skill.

Team building, management and other in-house programs

Try and do as many in-house training programs as you can. These should be useful things like computer training, time management, new technologies or something relevant to your industry. In the main, management training courses will teach you lots of great things about managing people, but they are not very useful if you don't like people. I know a manager who has done at least five of these courses, but they have not changed her management technique at all as she still believes she knows everything and everybody else knows nothing. Unfortunately, they cannot teach humility, lateral thinking, politeness and an unemotional viewpoint untainted by ego in a management course. You either have an egalitarian point of view or you don't.

As for team-building exercises, they are a questionable activity. They usually require you to do horrific things like touching people, sometimes by holding hands or massaging their necks. Any group activity which requires touching people you don't know, and probably don't like, should be avoided. Or they require you to stand in a circle and fall towards the earth, waiting for people to catch you, which is supposed to inspire trust in your colleagues. Of course they're going to catch you when everybody else is watching, but that doesn't mean they won't let you crash to the ground later on. (And put the boot in, just to be on the safe side.)

You can try these exercises but it is unlikely that they will change the way anybody thinks in any way whatsoever. They are only tools for people who do not know how to get on with other people in a reasonable way. Showing people which tools to use doesn't mean they will grasp the reasons why they are using them.

WHO IS MY AUDIENCE?

Remember who you're working for. Firstly, there's yourself, then there's your direct report (followed by his/her boss) and finally, the customer. Sometimes, the first two can overwhelm the last one, which is the most important. What happens then is that you gradually start forgetting the ultimate reason for the existence of your job and become obsessed with political twaddle. It might be worthwhile to stick up some useful epigrams in your office, such as 'The Customer Pays My Salary' or 'It's A Great Idea, But Will It Sell More Videos/Ratchet Wrenches/Rivets?' or whatever it is.

MAKE ALLIES NOT ENEMIES

Just as one should end one's life with a couple of good mates, one should have made a couple of worthwhile enemies as well. If you have no enemies at all it means you're probably just too damn nice and have spent too much time placating people. If you have too many enemies, it means that you have some sort of personality disorder.

The eminent Australian writer Patrick White had a late-life enemy in the Australian painter Sidney Nolan. Over the years they exchanged irascible public comments turning simple disagreements into legendary arguments full of bile and venom. (Nolan on White: 'I'm a good hater . . . I'll bury him . . . He doesn't understand much about life, does he? He's just lived with a man for 40 years.' White on Nolan: 'He's done far more harm to himself than he has to me. But anyway, he will bite the dust. He already has, as far as his talent goes.') Now this kind of exchange is almost worth staying alive for.

Enemies are best viewed from a distance, where you can see them in context and, with the benefit of hindsight, in a thoughtful and motivating fashion. What you don't want to do is make an instant enemy in your current job, particularly of somebody who holds a more powerful position. You will probably lose any struggle in a contest, unless you have made several worthwhile allies with power. The aim here is to make allies of those who will support you in a crisis or when you're trying to launch a new idea. Therefore, you should:

- Establish a relationship of trust, honesty and fairness with them by meeting deadlines, involving them in projects, giving credit when it's due and so on.
- Appeal to the aspects of their character that you know have the upper hand (see 'Sussing out other people's agendas'). Will the project you are trying to launch have kudos attached to it? Appeal to the person who is motivated by glory more than money.
- Appeal to their better nature (if they have one) — things like fairness, justice, equality.
- If an opportunity arises to support them in a moment of crisis, do so. This is an IOU and means they'll probably be compelled to support you in a similar instance.

True Crimes — Real Life Story

While working as a promotions assistant for a large record company Daniel, 27, had suspicions concerning his boss, a recently employed female marketing director. Despite the fact that she wore beautifully cut designer jackets, called everybody 'darling' and smiled a lot (revealing perfectly straight, white teeth of which she could justly be proud) he harboured dark thoughts about her essential character.

He noticed that she used her charm to inveigle people into working late to reach easily achievable deadlines. (As compensation, they received a bottle of French champagne each.) He noticed that she received flowers and gifts from industry colleagues (all of whom were men). He noticed that she went drinking regularly with the managing director, often turning up for work the next day much the worse for wear after imbibing one too many Long Island Iced Teas. He noticed that she took all the credit and none of the blame. She was a fraud, he decided. A phoney. He even started thinking her teeth might be fake.

'She used the "divide and conquer" tactic to great effect,' observes Daniel. 'Because she was the boss, we all trusted her automatically. We believed that she must be competent, because otherwise why would she be employed? She had a neat trick of confiding things to you, leading you to believe that it was the general incompetence of another person which caused things to go wrong. Everybody thought she was their best friend. Except me. I was the first person to work with her when she came on board, and I knew what she was like. It wasn't just her manner — my instinct bore out my observations.'

Daniel resigned from the company under a cloud: he had confided some of his fears to his colleagues, who couldn't believe that what he was saying might be true. They thought he was a bit wrong in the head.

'A year later, I received a phone call from a person I used to work with. She said that they eventually realised what the marketing director was up to when they all got together one day and exchanged stories that had been told to them in confidence. They elected two representatives who petitioned the managing director. They refused to accept her authority and gave him two choices: sack all of them or sack her.

'He sacked her,' finishes Daniel in a tone of great satisfaction. 'I was vindicated.'

There are two morals in this heartening story. One is that Daniel's initial instinct was correct. He felt he shouldn't trust this woman and his observations confirmed everything he felt. The other is that being right doesn't necessarily mean you'll be rewarded in your career.

'The best thing of all,' says Daniel, 'was that they finally checked out her CV. It was a pack of lies. She'd made up the whole thing.'

Looking, talking and acting smart

seven

'I think I'll wear it to the meeting. It frightens the editors. I'm the only one with Chanel couture. Let them kiss my buttons.' PATSY STONE, ABSOLUTELY FABULOUS

This section will tell you how to use your natural assets to get ahead a lot more quickly. The correct dress, grooming and attitude is your camouflage. You look and act like everybody else — that means you're just as capable as everybody else. It doesn't matter that you go home, put on that green sequined number hiding in the back of the closet and mime enthusiastically to Ethel Merman recordings in the safety of your lounge room. *They don't know that.* To them, you're just like one of them.

People talk a lot about 'image', but what they're actually talking about is the impression you make when you meet somebody. These images are grounded in our subconscious, hence the popularity of certain film stars. A basic film image is the idea of white and black: good versus evil. In films, since the early days of silents, 'good girls' were usually light-haired, 'evil women' were usually dark-haired. Blondes were round-eyed and innocent (Lillian Gish and Doris Day are good examples), dark-haired women had slanting eyes and were dangerous (Louise Brooks and Ava Gardner). Add to this cocktail of impressions an addictive dash of sexuality and you've got image.

Dress and attitude affect how people judge you even before they have any idea of your true potential. If you turn up for work wearing torn black jeans, boots and a snakeskin belt with a silver buckle depicting the words 'Live Hard, Die Young' then people will think you are either a drug addict or a musician. If you are either of these things, that's fine, but if you're a computer programmer with ambition, you won't get anywhere in the company. Conversely, if you turn up wearing a dress cut so low it looks like you caught your ankle on the straps as you were getting into it, six-inch heels and blood-red lipstick, you're destined to remain a budding actress forever. Nobody will take you seriously.

It's worthwhile making an effort because people like doing things with attractive people. You don't have to look like Cindy Crawford, you just have to make sure you tweak those hairs out of your moles. (If you don't tweak them people will become fascinated by them and will look at them rather than listen to what you are saying.)

Wearing no make-up and your hair pulled back severely from your head will lead everyone to believe that you are humourless and, possibly, a lesbian. Why make life difficult for yourself? It doesn't matter if you are a lesbian, it's nobody's business what you do in your own personal life, but we don't want to broadcast a negative perception that may boomerang against you and impede your progress. We have not yet reached a perfect world, unfortunately, and there are still a lot of old codgers on the brink of retirement in positions of power who hold ridiculous ideas about the way people should look and what they should do with their lives. Until they die you are never going to change their opinions. The world doesn't work that fast. Find another job, or be smart about it.

All work clothes are designed to be, and should be, slightly uncomfortable. After all, you're not at home lying on the couch. Good work clothes help to keep you alert and a little bit formal. If you want to get somewhere, the crucial thing to remember is: *dress and act for the position above you.*

WOMEN

It's true that women have to be organised to look as good as they do when they finally hit the office. They have to pluck those stray hairs as well as worrying about their make-up and nails. Look at the person above you. This person has more power and, presumably, more money than you. How do they dress? Do they teeter around the office on six-inch platforms wearing skimpy jersey tops? Do they wear tight sarong skirts and great clodhopping shoes? No, they don't. They wear a suit.

The suit

There are suits and then there are suits. A good suit is cut properly, it hangs properly and it has lining. (Lining is the stuff that ensures that when you take the skirt off, it doesn't look like you're still standing in it. No outline remains of your stomach that sticks out or your bottom that hangs down.)

You will need several of these suits, at least three so that you can choose bits from each one and each combination looks like a different suit. You'll have to accept that you will have to spend money if they are to last and not go out of fashion. Opt for the classic styles rather than the extremely fashionable ones.

There is the everyday, ordinary suit and then there is the Scare the Hell out of Them Suit. The latter is classified as a dangerous weapon and is to be used for very important meetings, performance reviews and any disciplinary action. The Scare the Hell out of Them Suit is at its best when you know you are going to be involved in an ugly scene with either your boss or the MD. When you walk in, people automatically flatten themselves against the walls. Wear the shortest skirt and the highest heels you can find with it and go get 'em.

The blouse

The only time you ever wear anything that opens to the navel is when you forget to do up your pyjamas. People do not want to see your cleavage, or worse, your lack of cleavage. You can wear bodysuits, but only if you don't take your jacket off. They are a bit too casual for professional wear. Floppy sleeves are cute, but not when you drag them in your bolognaise over a work lunch. Keep a plain white or black blouse (a colour that goes with everything you own) in your work space just in case there is an accident (spilt coffee, beer or somebody's blood) with the blouse you happen to be wearing.

Accessories

Clanky jewellery is out. Earrings that fall below your shoulder are also out. Turn the wrong way too quickly and you could put out somebody's eye with the flying earring missile. (Hair that has been sprayed to the consistency of cement can also do this.) Too many rings can cause problems when you shake hands with somebody as bits of skin can be caught agonisingly between them.

Handbags should not be large and unwieldy, should be made of good leather and preferably black. Keep shoes to a reasonable 2 to 3 cm heel; pumps in a variety of colours are best. Wear the mega-heels when you have a VIP meeting and there are lots of short men who want to have a go at you. You can then tower over them and intimidate them while getting closer to the height of the taller men. (Note:

never wear white shoes. Ever. People will think you either spend time in a psychiatric ward or are Minnie Mouse.) Also keep several spare pairs of stockings in your desk so you're not caught out.

Make-up
Just because electric blue eye shadow is back in fashion doesn't mean you have to wear it. Let's face it, it was only barely acceptable on seventies popstars, and the only person who could wear it without looking like she'd walked into a doorhandle was Agnetha Faltskog, the beautiful blonde from ABBA. (She is also the only person in the known universe who could wear the instantly ugly-making 'flicks' where the fringe is 'flicked' from either side of a central part.) If you are going to wear blusher, try not to wander around like a kewpie doll with two bright round spots of colour on your cheeks. Don't bother with 'the seasons' changing colours', it's just another way for make-up companies to make money; find out what suits you and stick to it.

Fashion no-nos
Blue eye shadow
White shoes
White shoes with black stockings
Pink dots of blush
Green/pink hair
Dots and stripes together
White clothes under which you can see your underwear
Platform shoes
Obvious pantyline
Tattoos
Black lipstick and nail polish
Long red frightening talons masquerading as nails

Green teeth

Flat shoes (you look like you're standing in a pile of dirt)

Flat shoes with long, flared skirts

Boob tubes

Suede shoes

Velvet or (worse) velour

Corduroy and gingham

Anything shirred

Cotton skirts and wool stockings (don't mix your seasons)

Sequins

Diamantés

Anything with a brand name or writing on it, unless it is your company T-shirt

Halter-tops

MEN

Outside of work, there are lots and lots of acceptable things for men to wear, but work attire largely depends on yourself and your industry. You may not have to wear a tie if you can get away with a linen suit and polo-neck jumper or skivvy. That can look effective, but it sits better in an arty-farty industry. Flares have recently made a comeback (much to the horror of those of us who were forced into wearing these clothes in our extreme youth) but if you're going to wear them you really have to wear the full garb: flared jacket, collars that reach to your shoulder, body shirts, a wide, loud tie and platform shoes. Do you really want to wear all that?

It's true, I know a man who wears spats to work, occasionally. But then, he also wears a sharply cut pin-striped suit and a hat. These are period clothes and don't look any good without all the other bits. They were designed that way: that is the essence of style. Style does not,

I repeat not, consist of shorts, a short-sleeved shirt and tie, long socks and shoes. If anybody designed this it was the Old Boffo publican in Cairns.

If you think style is something you jump over, then the best thing you can do is stick to the ordinary suit. The only time you don't have to wear the suit is on the corporate 'civvies' day. Try not to look like a complete dork on this day by wearing what are known as 'matched separates', usually bought by the wife or mother. These are unbelievably uncool, although far more acceptable than ripped jeans and a T-shirt displaying the legend 'Shut Up Bitch'. Overall, dress on this day as though you are taking somebody out for dinner.

The suit

Hang on to your wallet, because you're going to have to spend a fair bit of money and get a good one. There is a huge difference between the $99 suit and the $1500 suit. The difference is in the cut and the cloth. Not that you have to spend $1500 because you can purchase suits at a discount and get one for a reasonable price. If you don't know what you are doing then go conservative. If you want to buy separates, choose black, dark green or dark blue pants. Brightly coloured suits should be avoided unless you really know what you are doing as they don't suit everybody and you have to have a particular type of personality to carry it off. Don't ever buy anything brown. There is no excuse for suits that are too tight, too large or too long in the pants or sleeves. Spend some money and get them altered.

Shirts

Never wear a patterned shirt because unless you purchase a suitable kind people will constantly approach you trying to lay a bet, apart from the altogether separate problem of what kind of tie to wear with it (there is a strong possibility that the person with the patterned shirt has also a large selection of patterned ties). White is best, but if you have a tendency to slop things all over yourself, dark blue or green shirts are preferable. A black shirt, although brilliant for dirt, will make you look like a priest or an undertaker and these two types, though worthy in themselves, do tend to make people nervous.

Shirts have to endure a great deal of wear and tear, particularly around the collar and cuffs, and should be a thick cotton or blend thereof. If you purchase a polyester, synthetic or body shirt, don't wear it — use it to light the barbeque instead. They just do not breathe effectively. Good shirts also have a stiffened or lined collar, with little bits of plastic in the ends of the collar. If you don't have these, the collar will curl up at the edges making you look rather like a depressed elf who has been drizzled on.

Try not to get too excited and buy the shirts which come in packs of 12 dozen for ten bucks. They look like a great deal, but actually give the impression that you are dressed in cling-wrap. People can see your body. And let's face it: we don't really want them to, do we? Even if you have a body like Arnold Schwarzenegger's it may be a distraction, resulting in people signing the wrong bits of paper, and, possibly, causing car accidents.

There are two schools of thought about what to wear under the white shirt: the T-shirt or the singlet. The rule is: wear a white T-shirt under a white shirt and a singlet under coloured shirts. Never wear short-sleeved shirts unless you are a raffle-ticket seller for the local RSL. Always roll the sleeves of your long shirt up to just below the elbow if the airconditioning isn't working, otherwise live with it. If your shirt starts fraying at the crucial edges, developing the fur-ball disease, looks like the moths have had a regular party on it, or has that distinctive grease stain, throw it away and buy a new one. One cannot afford to be cheap with one's shirts.

As to vests, they have to be chosen very carefully before they can be worn, and anything that was knitted by an aged, though well-meaning, relative, is definitely out. Always remember to leave the bottom button of the vest undone. This innovative style was created by King Henry VIII as he was too fat to do the bottom button up, hence it became the fashion.

A word on ironing: it is a good idea to iron the shirt. If you are wearing a vest one need only iron the collar, sleeves and cuffs. Otherwise, you'll have to iron the whole thing. If you can't be bothered ironing then have your shirts starched, but not so often that they are liable to crack and disintegrate into a thousand tiny pieces upon touching.

Ties

This is about the only garment in which a man can express his personality. But you don't want to express the personality of a sexist, beer-swilling yobbo by wearing a tie with a naked woman decorated with little coloured lights in the appropriate places. Save that tie for the Moose's Head in the Trough annual dinner.

Ties should be silk and real, consisting of a length of cloth. Ties attached to a piece of elastic are simply not acceptable under any circumstances. Any pattern will do, as long as it's not fluorescent or has pictures of cartoon characters on it. Yeah, sure we know they're fun, but you'll just look like a desperate salesman who hisses to people as they walk by: 'Hey, lady, wanna buy a cheap watch?' while ominously opening his overcoat. In a recent US study, yellow was deemed to be the colour of success but that doesn't include a large blow-up of Bart Simpson's cunning mug. Cravats and string ties are out. You're not the Dauphin ('My father, the King!'), and you're not going line-dancing. Unless you are an architect, scientist or an academic we do not recommend bow ties as one tends to look a little like a lurid game-show presenter.

As to tying the tie there are about a thousand knots from which you can choose, but the Windsor and the slipknot are the most common. Make it look a reasonable shape and not like a teeny-weeny spaghetti knot above which your head balloons, purple and bulging and larger than life. Do not loosen the tie when in the office under any circumstances. When tied, the bottom of the tie should be touching your belt buckle, not hovering somewhere near your armpits or your crotch. Never undo the top button of your shirt while you are still wearing a tie. If it's too tight around the neck then buy a new, larger shirt. When wearing a tie, make sure the collar of your shirt covers it at the back. Keep a spare shirt in your work space along with a spare pair of socks.

Shoes, socks and belts

White shoes are out. Are you getting married? No, and even if you are you shouldn't wear them, as it seems the only person who could really get away with it was Elvis Presley. Make them leather and good in black or very dark brown. If they're not leather then you will have problems with that odorous condition beloved of podiatrists known as Stinky Foot. Stinky Foot is not usually a problem until you come home and overpower your partner with it (that's actually the reason they faint at the front door, you know) but you may just have a whole pile of traditional Japanese clients and they're not wrinkling up their noses in imitation of a smile.

Socks contribute largely to this condition. Socks should be 100 per cent cotton or wool and should match your shoes, just as your shoes should match your belt. Belts should also be made of leather or a very good equivalent. Buckles should not be large, otherwise they will draw attention to a much-beloved part of your person. Socks and sandals should never be worn under any circumstances whatsoever. If you do see anyone wearing these, please send their name and address to the author — she will ensure they are whipped on the back of the legs with a wet tea-towel until suitably chastened.

Jewellery and accessories

Anything that makes people think you may be part of an overseas revue is out. Cufflinks, tiepin and a good watch are all heartily recommended. So too a good wallet and attaché case, but they should be of the same colour. Never be cheap with a pen — it looks wrong, somehow, if you are dressed to the nines and then pull out some ratty old biro with a chewed top. If you favour an earring then make sure it's small and discreet. More than one is not recommended. A wedding ring is recommended if you want people to know that you are married.

Fashion no-nos

Black pants with a brown belt
Western shirts
Cravats or string ties
Anything mesh or leather (except shoes and belts)
Cardigans
Anything brown or tan
Too-tight vests or jumpers knitted by one's mother
Bright green jumper knitted by one's mother

Platform shoes

Wide ties

Frocks

Old School Tie (only useful if the boss is wearing the same one)

White socks (you have to be wearing white shoes and we've already said they're out)

Blouson jackets

Cartoon characters

Nose hair or ear hair — for God's sake, trim it

Sandshoes or Hush Puppies

Striped shirts with striped ties

Thongs

Tank-tops

Shorts

Tattoos

Football socks — who cares if they won the premiership?

GROOMING

Although tousled hair looks great in fashion photos, it is not a good idea going into work looking as if you just got out of bed. Keep it simple and in a reasonable colour spectrum. Nothing that will scare your clients, customers or work colleagues. Snowfall can be taken care of by an anti-dandruff shampoo.

If you're growing a beard, grow it during the holidays or people will think you've been on the tiles for a couple of days. If you have been on the tiles, use Visine. Trim all unwanted hair growth: nose, ear and moles. Make an effort to have more than one eyebrow.

It is not necessary for men to wear aftershave, particularly if it smells like you spent an hour or two in the pig shed. Unless it's subtle and good (read expensive) don't bother with it. Wear deodorant. This might be obvious but some people don't, you know. If people take a step or two backwards when you stand near them, it probably isn't because they are awed by your presence. It's probably because you stink.

True Crimes — Real Life Story

As the only female manager in the history of her company, Alison, 33, found that not only did her presence raise the ire of numerous men with entrenched attitudes in the company, but that the women came to her with all sorts of longstanding issues that they hoped she would be able to solve.

'You wouldn't believe the problems that these women had,' says Alison. 'First there was the extremely trivial issue of one of the blokes allegedly opening one of my female staff's letters. This juvenile issue was insoluble because it was a personality clash: he was keen on her but she wouldn't have a bar of him. They even poked their tongues out at each other during the meeting.

'Following hot on the heels of this riveting clash, was the day the administration manager came to me about the sanitary napkin containers in the bathroom. Apparently, people had been putting other things in there. Naturally, I was intrigued as to what these unnamed things could be, so I said: "What? You mean empty takeaway Chinese containers?" I was joking, but she said "yes", somebody had! Then I had to talk to every single woman in the company about it, just to "remind" them.

'But the dooziest issue of all was this one. There was one woman in the company who had a body odour problem. It was so severe that when she sat on a chair nobody else could bear to sit on it and they had to get a new one. Her personal hygiene really wasn't very good. Part of the problem was that she didn't dry her clothes properly, so you can imagine. It got to the point where the warehouse manager, a very direct, kind man, lodged what can only be termed an "official" complaint with me in a discreet corner of the warehouse one day.

'The onus was on me to do something about it. His was not the only complaint. I would have to say that this was without doubt the most difficult thing I have had to do in my entire career. Sacking a person is bad, but not as bad as this. I got her into my office on some other pretext and pretended that it was just me that had noticed, so she wouldn't be embarrassed. I started off with a general discussion and gradually led up to the fact that it might be holding her back in her career. I tried to behave like the family doctor and was very sympathetic and kind about it. She was mortified. She cried. But what can you say? It was awful.

'Even though things were understandably cool between us for a while, there were no further complaints.'

ATTITUDE

Over and above everything else attitude will get you through. On a bad day, which is when you'll need it most, attitude can masquerade as confidence. Attitude will keep everybody firmly in their respective places. You'll notice that men have heaps more attitude than women, usually. Your average man thinks automatically that he is just as good as everybody else, whereas your average woman thinks she has to earn her stripes. If you're feeling a little bit insecure start cultivating some attitude. Never let anybody know you're feeling this way. Anybody who gets even the slightest hint of it will exploit you until you explode.

Body talk

The way you carry yourself conveys a message just as much as anything else. The actress Marilyn Monroe was plagued by chronic insecurity all her life, but you would never have known it from the way she carried herself in public. 'I would walk very slowly and turn my head, as if I was a little Queen', she was quoted as saying.

Pull your head up and your shoulders back. Walk in there as if you own the joint. Head tilted back slightly but not too far. You want to appear only slightly superior, not as if you just smelled something bad. Look everybody in the eye as you cruise through the office. Either say 'hello' or nod 'hello'. (The nod seems to have a more professional tinge, for some reason.) This is never more important than when you're under fire. Do you want them to think you're cowed? Never! Haven't you got any pride? Even if you're losing the battle, get the attitude going big time and say 'good morning' to everybody in your usual fashion. Don't avoid people. It may even rattle them a bit: they'll be thinking 'God, she's in the worst professional trouble she's ever been in in her whole career and look at her! You'd never think so.'

With your head back, smile. But don't show your teeth. I mean, they're not a friend of yours, are they? Do you like them? No, of course you don't. The closed mouth smile is the one to use. That way, you appear friendly but not as if you can be taken advantage of. Walk with purpose. Not too slow and not too fast. Never run. Only once, in my whole career, have I seen anyone run. Once. They were sent away for a little rest shortly afterwards.

If you do this, people may level the charge of arrogance at you. So what? Arrogance is a most underrated quality. All it means is that you know what you're capable of, you know what you're doing and you know where you're going. What's the matter with that? Let's face it: you're going to have to bang your own drum, because nobody in the known universe could possibly be unselfish enough to do it for you. (Apart from your friends and you've got enough on them to make it seem like a fair exchange.) After all, men have had this charge levelled against them for centuries and look where it got them! It's better than being called 'incompetent' or 'ineffectual' or 'a big flossy', isn't it?

What are they really thinking?

This kind of worrying seems to affect women more than men. Men commonly either don't notice or don't care. They know they're great, whereas criticism works away on a woman's confidence and esteem like mould. Who cares? Do you really care? You only have to get on with these people while you're at work, you don't have to see them at any other time. Who cares what they think! So you overheard what you thought was somebody bitching about you in the corridor. Save your worrying for the people who really matter: your friends and your family. It matters what they think of you. Forget everybody else. Besides, it's much better to be talked about than talked over.

ETIQUETTE

There are conventional standards in corporate life and it makes no sense alienating people by failing to observe proprieties that put them at their ease. There are some people who are masters at making other people feel uncomfortable. A classic way of putting somebody in their place is to bark 'Come!' without lifting your head when they knock on the door, and leave them standing there shuffling uncertainly until you've finished whatever it is you're doing.

(Only use this with underlings who are really being difficult and who will never pose a threat to you.)

Here are some hints about everyday office etiquette:

The telephone

Don't hang around somebody's office door while they're on the phone, or stand glaring at them in front of their desk when you want something answered. They can see you. They haven't been instantly smitten with blindness. As soon as they've finished the call, they'll come around and see what it is you want. (This is a favourite action of the Control Freak who wants people to be constantly at her beck and call.)

If somebody does this to you, ignore them. Smile at them to acknowledge their presence but keep talking until you legitimately finish the call. Draw it out for a couple of minutes if you have to, just to make the point. If you are in an informal meeting and the phone rings, leave the office. Don't sit there listening to the whole thing. Do you really want to watch somebody collapse with anxiety at the results of their STD test?

The knock

Always knock on office doors. Don't just barge in. The person you want to see may be so absorbed in what they are doing that they haven't noticed you hanging about. The knock alerts them to your presence. Follow this with 'Excuse me for interrupting, but do you have a couple of minutes?' Never sit down without being invited to.

Looking through papers

Don't touch anything on anybody's desk, unless it's a magazine. This is the work equivalent of opening other people's mail and is extremely rude. You can look of course, and if you've mastered the art of reading things upside-down good luck to you, but just don't touch. Also, don't read the material that people have just put through the fax. People hate that.

The paper chase

There are two kinds of people in this world: spreaders and stackers. The former arrange their papers horizontally, the latter vertically. Spreaders can be a bit more of a problem because they move outwards in ever-growing circles, like a small explosion, and therefore tend to impinge on other people, particularly if they're not contained by an office but have imagined wider access in the workstation, while the stacker moves upwards. (The stacker can sometimes look as if they're in a paper prison, their little head peering out at you.) You will notice that MDs and senior management appear to be neither. That is because they make big-picture decisions which require less paper. But rest assured, inside every MD is an embryo spreader or stacker, just waiting for an opportunity to jump right out.

Unfortunately, there are still some old-fashioned people in this world who believe the old cliché 'a tidy desk is a tidy mind'. (They also believe that 'cleanliness is next to Godliness' and we know that isn't true.) Never trust people with totally clean desks, unless they're MDs. There is something suspicious about a pristine, dust-free desk supporting nothing but a pen and a photograph. It's eerie — like somebody died.

The old cliché is rubbish, of course, as there is absolutely no correlation between a tidy/untidy desk and a person's ability to do the job. In fact some spreaders have an astounding photographic memory and they can tell you exactly where that particular piece of paper is, buried under three files, a heavy report and 20 000 other bits of paper, which will amaze and astonish you. 'Now I remember that memo,' they will say, half to themselves. 'Just give me a second.' And you'll be thinking: 'How long do you want? A year?' and then they will dumbfound you by reaching down, under and around (rather like a magician) and triumphantly flourishing the exact memo in your face. (The only time spreaders are in real trouble is when they clean up their office. They can't find anything, after that.)

Stackers appear to be more organised, but aren't really. They just look neater. Try to maintain an even balance. If you're a spreader and your boss frowns when he walks into your office, then you'd better make a change. His or her perception is what's important here, remember?

Terms of endearment — addressing others

How you address people and the tone of voice that you use can be very effective in getting people on your side or making enemies. Americans have a wonderful way of conferring respect without looking like grovelling fools by using the words 'Sir' and 'Ma'am'. Absolutely everybody does it, from waiters to billionaire magnates. How do they do it? Something about their accent makes it inoffensive and impressive at the same time; how could one possibly take offence to James Stewart stammering 'Well, um, er . . . no ma'am'?

We in Australia are far too egalitarian to dream of mentioning these words, seeing them not only as evidence of our convict past but part and parcel of an attitude in which the sentiment 'Who the hell do they think they are, anyway?' figures prominently. It's a shame really, as the use of these words can give you the opportunity to say some outrageous things while appearing polite. When you disagree with somebody, preface your comment with 'With all due respect' or 'I understand your point of view, but . . . '. Other similar phrases to use can be found in the section 'Phrases that will get you out of trouble'.

The introduction

When you're introduced to somebody, smile at them and say 'Hello. How are you?' while sticking out your hand. Repeat their name. 'Hello. How are you, Dennis?' means that you are in less danger of forgetting their name if you have to introduce them to somebody else. On this occasion, you can then say: 'Joanne, this is Dennis. Dennis does some printing jobs for us.' Forgetting somebody's name is a perennial worry. Don't even attempt to make a stab at it hoping that by a lucky chance you may stumble on the right one. If you get it wrong you're going to look even sillier. All you have to do is say 'I'm sorry, I didn't catch your name', while looking unconcerned. If you've spent a long time working with somebody and six months later you run into them at a function and you can't remember their name, do either of the following: say 'Will you excuse me for a moment, I have to speak to XXX' and avoid them like the plague until you can find somebody who knows their name, or say 'I'm terribly sorry, your name seems to have escaped me. I have a mind packed full of trivialities. I even forget my own name sometimes. Dianne, not a hard name to forget.' (You say this to give them an escape route just in case they've forgotten yours.)

Deliberately forgetting somebody's name is a good trick to use when you want to deflate somebody. I know somebody who meets a mutual work acquaintance every quarter or so. He doesn't like him and although he remembers perfectly well who he is every time he meets him, he acts like it's the first time, leaving him with the uncomfortable sense that there is some problem as to his identity. 'You remember Acton, don't you?' 'Do I?' he says. 'Pleased to meet you,' while enthusiastically shaking the other's hand. Saying 'Who?' when conversation centres on somebody you all know gives everyone the signal that they are of no consequence. This is particularly useful if you are challenged by this person and so you have to convey that everybody is really making a great fuss over nothing. 'You remember, he did the brochures for us for the company dinner.' Then you can say, vaguely, 'Oh . . . yes'.

True Crimes — Real Life Story

The large bulk of senior management were grouped around the table having drinks. They were there to do business with relevant people in that state, so the heavies with all their charm were wheeled out at the insistence of the sales manager, John, 42, who was grinning heartily at his cleverness in getting them all there.

'One of our major clients, a man called Robert Plant, was sitting next to me,' says John. 'He seemed very happy — all that had stopped us before from finalising the biggest deal we had yet done with him was that he had felt the company didn't "care" enough about him. The fact that the managing director and all of senior management was there seemed to convince him of our seriousness.

'As I sat there, thinking about the new pool I would put in with the commission money, I heard our sales director talking to Robert. The sales director was a very nice, polite, circumspect man, with a storehouse of very boring stories. His way of managing uncomfortable social situations was to just ramble on. I could see Robert's eyes glazing over, but I was sitting on the other side of the charmed circle, so I couldn't get to him to rescue him. It would have looked too obvious. As I kept one ear on the conversation, I heard the sales director refer to Robert Plant, our best client, as Ralph. Everything he said he prefaced with the words "Well, Ralph ... blah, blah, blah". He must have done it at least 15 or 16 times in the ten minutes I was listening.

'All the other senior management were smiling politely, as they were very aware that the man's name was not Ralph. I waited for somebody to say something, but nobody did. It's hard sometimes to get a word in when the sales director is in the middle of telling a story about gum trees or fencing or whatever. Obviously, the situation couldn't go on.

'A deadly silence fell except for the sales director from whom the name "Ralph" kept echoing with depressing repetition. Finally our managing director, unable to stand it any longer, leaned over and, interrupting without preamble, said: "I'm sorry. But I thought your name was Robert. Is it Robert or Ralph?" And everybody said in unison "Robert!" including Robert himself.

'And the Managing Director said: "I thought so. I was beginning to doubt myself because nobody said anything!" and Robert/Ralph said: "I quite like Ralph as a name, anyway" and everybody laughed. But it was excruciating while it went on.'

Small talk

This is always a nightmare. You need to make some effort here if you are to make a good impression. It's boring and a total waste of time as you'll never have a really interesting conversation but you should leave people with the impression that you *are* genuinely interested.

If you're stuck with somebody for only a couple of minutes (an overseas visitor for instance) who is being introduced to everybody around the office, you probably only have to muster up a couple of sentences. 'Are you going to try and play the tourist a bit while you are here?' is better than 'Is this your first trip?'. You can then recommend various places to go to, which can keep you safely talking for up to ten minutes. Think up a few questions of this type at home and practise them so that you can use them whenever you're put on the spot.

Longer times, like dinners, require more effort. Try to get a bit of an idea who the person is and what they do. Then you can find out what topics to avoid. Never talk about yourself. Talk about them, then they will think you are amazingly charming. Don't talk about sex, politics, religion, health or diseases. They are exceedingly dull topics. Current affairs, recent news, the media, celebrities, books and films, television, travel, music and sport are all excellent. (Bad service is also a good one, as you can tell several humorous anecdotes.) If you read newspapers and magazines then you should be able to converse on these topics without fear. Ask questions ('What do you think of pay TV?') but never ask any personal questions unless they bring them up, in which case you should confine yourself to nodding.

Don't bother with all the uncomfortable um-ing and ah-ing just after you are introduced but fix them with your eye, choose an appropriate topic and launch straight into it. 'Did you see *Melrose Place* last week?' is a sure-fire winner, as you can lead straight into television-viewing habits and all other forms of popular culture which can keep you going for hours and hours.

THE PLOTTING AND SCHEMING CHECKLIST

The way you dress, look and act conditions the way you are perceived in the company. The following list should be helpful to you if you need to lift your game in this respect. You should do this if you feel, instinctively, that things are not going well, or you have received one warning memo. If you have received your second warning memo and people are beginning to avoid you, you can still use these techniques, but it might be wise to start looking for another job, just in case.

- Make a list of everybody who is difficult to work with. Work out what motivates them and make a conscious effort to get on their good side. Do this by supporting them openly in a meeting, helping them with a project or asking for their opinion or advice.
- Examine your wardrobe. Does it need overhauling? Buy some clothes for the position above you.
- Pay compliments to everybody — even those you loathe and despise. Most people are polite enough to feel that they should repay these at some later date. Being nice will get you further than being nasty.
- Dump all those people you are friendly with who are either beneath your current position or gossips.
- Start cultivating those people who are above you in status and power.
- Work out who is your worst enemy. Work out a devilish strategy to lower their reputation and with luck, get them out of the company. It's either you or them.
- Use the Window of Opportunity and other defensive techniques at every opportunity.
- Be seen having lunch at your desk. Arrive early and leave late.
- If you're a spreader or a stacker, tidy up your office.

- Go out for post-work drinks or dinner with your colleagues. Try and get as much information out of them as you can.
- Use the lamington bribe as soon as possible. Chat to people while you hand them out.

What to do when things go horribly wrong

eight

'No Lisa, we don't go on strike . . . we just go to work and do everything in a half-arsed fashion.' HOMER SIMPSON

This section of the book will help you not only to avoid, but to extricate yourself from, any nasty work situations if they occur. It deals with legal protection, defensive techniques and methods of attack. If you have absorbed the information in prior sections, then there will be less chance of something horrific happening. But, hey, everybody makes mistakes, or as they say in Workspeak, 'ill-advised decisions'.

UGLY SCENES

Work is full of ugly scenes. An ugly scene is classified as anything in which Workspeak is not used to its full potential. In these instances, a raw, blatant form of speech called Direct English is used. Ugly scenes proliferate when you are under fire and if you just stand there with your mouth open, aghast with apprehension, the inevitable result will be that you are comprehensively done over.

Ugly scenes happen when you have accidentally stepped on somebody's turf, are being challenged by your minion subordinates, or accused of any type of unprofessional behaviour in a public fashion. The first ugly scenes begin with the warning memo and the last ones end with you emptying your desk. In between are several ugly scenes of such horror and intensity that you think you have stumbled into a surrealistic Salvador Dali painting. They consist of the 'attitude speech', another warning memo, several meetings behind closed doors and long and agonising performance reviews.

DEFENSIVE TECHNIQUES

The aim here is to squash, totally and completely, anybody who is plotting and scheming against you. It's got to be contained, and it's got to be done well, so that the enemy is vanquished utterly. You've got to put people in their places so thoroughly that they will never challenge you again. Lying, plotting and scheming, and attitude are the weapons in your defensive armoury. Use them absolutely. Guilt, pity and mercy are emotions you cannot allow yourself to feel. Think of yourself as a military commander. Who are your allies? Cultivate them. Who are your enemies? Take no prisoners and don't give them an opportunity to have a go at you. If you have to have a go at somebody, there are many tried and true techniques to employ. But you have to do all of this while appearing to be fair and just.

Character assassination

This is remarkably easy to do. Go straight to the nearest gossip and confidentially tell them some horrific story about the person you want to get. It doesn't matter whether it's true or not, and most people won't believe it, but throw enough mud and some of it sticks. The whole idea here is to throw a big fat question mark over that person, which will hover there like the Sword of Damocles. If you haven't jumped up and down over every little thing that goes wrong and haven't been injudicious and indiscreet, then the chances of people believing you will be even greater. The office gossip will be forever grateful to you — she's been dying for you to open up a bit and now you are! All you have to do is say you thought it was them going into the Hell Fire Club dressed in a leather truss and carrying a whip. You didn't say it *was* them, you only said you *thought* it was them.

Lying

Use this one at all opportunities. No, you didn't receive that memo. No, you don't know anything about that project deadline. It was only a conversation and there's nothing on paper. You (or they) must have misheard. No, you don't know anything about that public relations disaster. That wasn't your project. No, no, no. You know nothing.

Threatening

This one is most effective, but is to be used very, very discreetly. Never have any witnesses to a standover tactic. Let's say you're the assistant to the marketing manager but you have an enemy: the assistant to the administration manager. She has a marketing degree and she secretly thinks she would make a much better assistant to the marketing manager than you would. So far, she has managed to use character assassination and lying to undermine you. You've tried all the fair and just tactics but you are at your wits' end at what to do — you feel she is winning the battle.

What you can do is walk to the bus-stop with her, or use the pretext of: 'Would you like to have a drink after work?' It doesn't matter where you corner her — if it's in the middle of the car park so much the better. Then, you say something like this: 'Now, you listen to me. I know exactly what you're doing and I know why you're doing it. All I have to say to you is don't mess with me because I swear to God I will make you suffer for it in ways you can't even imagine. I'm smarter than you and I'm better at this than you and you will rue the day you ever messed with me. Because I will make sure that if I go down, you'll be going down as well,' or words to that effect.

Then you sit back and see what happens. If she says you threatened her, deny it. 'I don't know what the woman's talking about,' you can say, 'As if I would do something like that. How ridiculous!' Or even better, 'I'm amazed. Truly amazed. We get on so well. I can't believe she would accuse me of such things. I'm horrified! Horrified and saddened. I had no idea there were any problems between us. Naturally, if I thought there were any, I would be the first person to want to assist in fixing them. I would never, ever do such a thing!' But you've got to be prepared to carry out your threat if the behaviour doesn't stop.

The confession

Never own up to a major stuff-up. Never say 'I made a mistake'. What you say is: 'There must have been a communication problem'. What you can own up to are small, insignificant stuff-ups. People will respect you not only for taking responsibility for an action of yours (the stuff of which future managers are made) but also for owning up to a small stuff-up, and are therefore more likely to believe you when you say that the mortifying debacle that lost the company one of its biggest clients was not your fault.

(In many respects, you're probably right as giant mistakes are usually the result of bad communication and therefore involve more than one person.)

A small stuff-up is something like getting the in-house company newsletter out two days late. But you still don't say you made a mistake. What you say is: 'I take full responsibility for this, but I feel compelled to point out that on the day that it was due the photocopier exploded'. (You may also want to add: 'I'm not using this as an excuse, it's just a reason'.) It doesn't matter what the reason is, just think of something without blaming anybody. If you can't think of a good excuse ('reason' in Workspeak) then confine yourself to stating: 'I take full responsibility for this'. Of course, they may then say to you: 'You should have been better prepared. If you had been running to schedule, then you could have used the photocopying company up the road and still met your deadline', in which case you then say: 'Yes, I understand' and leave the room.

Pointing the finger

This is never a good thing to do unless you're really stuck. It's a very low act and you have to be on the verge of chewing off your own hand through desperation to do it. If the person is a tried and true enemy then letting them take the blame for something you did is still a low act, but can have a rejuvenating effect on your enemy, like a low-voltage electric shock. They will take careful note of the fact that you are still around.

Pretending to be really, really nice

This is an excellent tool to use. This is when you present yourself as being so nice, so fair and so just that nobody in their right mind could think that you were capable of low acts like lying, threatening or setting somebody up. The last thing you want is for people to think that you might be capable of such deeds or for them to start looking at you with suspicion. Never comment on anybody's personality no matter how bad it may be. If somebody accuses you of something, say 'I'm shocked!' or 'I had no idea people could say such horrid things', with your lip trembling ever so slightly. Or you can try just shaking your head and sighing, pityingly — much more eloquent than a stream of words.

Ruling through fear — the bend-over technique

Whether you are in management, have just been elevated to management or are hoping, one day, to be in management, you will find that some people are happy to work with you while others are equally blissful at the prospect of working against you. What you've got to do is work out the best way of approaching people. Will they respond to praise or a challenge? Do they like feeling wanted and showered with warm fuzzies? Do they consider a fair exchange for working long hours and on weekends is a long lunch every quarter? Are they ultimately bigheads, believing nobody does anything better than they do? Do they have an attitude problem? Sometimes, the only way of dealing with a person like this is to rule through fear.

They might have had a dominating mother and considered joining either the army or a nunnery, and perhaps did, only to discover that these institutions didn't really appreciate their unique individual qualities. Either way, the only way to manage them is to tell them what to do firmly and finally. Use a toned-down version of the wearing-down process and every fortnight or so, at any vague signs of rebellion, tell them to bend over and stick a difficult project or 'attitude speech' right where the sun don't shine. You want them to quiver with fear at the mere sound of your steel-capped boot or stiletto heel approaching their office door.

Number crunching

In politics, people are employed especially to work out who is going to cross the floor on a crucial issue. You don't need to employ anybody, as you have already done all the schmoozing you need. It's only in situations of potential danger that all the knowledge of people's personalities that you have stored inside that head of yours becomes useful. If you're relatively smart, you should be able to work out who is going to support you in a moment of crisis. It's useful to know their motivation too — people are too unpredictable to put firmly into a box — because it may suit them to support you one day but be totally against you on another occasion.

Planting mines

This is a very clever and witty ploy with the same kind of effect as a practical joke. Good practical jokes make you want to stick around to see the reaction. When you plant a mine you may still want to hang around to see bits of dismembered bodies sailing past you, but you don't know exactly when the mine is going to be stepped on. Its only drawback is that it's a bit random. Mines are excellent to plant if you are forced into leaving the company but you want to leave somebody with a parting gift as they impressed you so much. Assembling the bomb can include the omission button (where you neglect to tell somebody something important and they stuff up spectacularly) like 'forgetting' to mention that their favourite, only, must-tell joke (about Helen Keller's dog) won't go down really well with the overseas VIP, whose daughter is a deaf mute.

True Crimes — Real Life Story

John, 32, had recently left his company, an overseas-owned conglomerate which manufactured and sold window-hangings. As the marketing manager, he was responsible for promoting the wide range of venetian blinds, curtains, rods and hooks that the company made. At first, John says, the job was 'a great challenge' as the company's products and therefore its image were so dated that it looked like they sold opera dresses for eighteenth-century widows (not windows) a la *Hello, Dolly!*, and as for venetians, they had not yet come back into vogue and were associated with cheap, almost sordid, rental accommodation.

'Gradually, over a period of about 18 months, we picked up the pace and became a company to be reckoned with in the industry,' says John. 'Unfortunately, my boss, the marketing director, was also a force to be reckoned with. He was a Mr Credibility, and was always talking about the seventies. His clothes, I am convinced, were the same ones he wore in the seventies; you know, body shirts and Hush Puppies. He had a mass of curly, salt and pepper hair and a handlebar moustache, favoured by men who wore open-necked shirts and gold chains and chatted up women at discos when he was in his prime.

'Apart from being outmoded and outdated, his attitude was that nobody knew better than he did. He was a very strange man, always jumping from one topic to another like a firefly, nothing he said ever seemed logical and he was constantly changing his mind. Somebody in our office (I think it was the administration manager) diagnosed him as having ADD (Attention Deficit Disorder). I didn't care what he had — all I knew was that he was making my job very difficult. Decisions made on a whim, intense enthusiasm one day and morose apathy the next. He was a very strange man.

'Anyway, one thing led to another and after a series of ugly scenes, in which the managing director backed this lunatic up (they were old mates), I left the company. But my boss had made such an impression on me, that I felt I just had to leave him a parting gift, to show him just how much he meant to me.'

John planted a mine for his old boss, which, although it took a year to detonate, was immensely gratifying when it did finally explode. He sent every bodgy memo he had received from his boss, every story of harassment and victimisation from past employees and records of joke meetings (ambushes, for John) to the Head Office in New York, which he knew was looking closely at every overseas office.

'Everything I sent showed them the level of mateship and corruption there was in the higher echelons of the company,' he says. 'By protecting this man, the MD was tacitly approving a manner of work practice which was very unprofessional and extremely bad for the company in the long run.

'I knew it would take the heavies from overseas about a year to really focus on our operation. Next thing I heard was that my boss had "resigned" and the company was going into a major restructure. My sources told me that my little package to New York was a major part of the "restructuring" effort. I was immensely pleased about this and felt not one skerrick of guilt. They didn't treat me fairly and in the end, they suffered for it.'

John's story demonstrates that, in the end, particularly in private enterprise, those who make the wrong business decisions (for reasons of friendship or 'mateship') will be made accountable. When it comes, revenge is sweet.

Going for the jugular — the set-up

Never underestimate the enemy. There's no point in going for somebody if they only end up with a small cut over which they can put a bandaid. What you've got to do is make a great swipe for the jugular so that there's an enormous pool of blood on the floor, and so that they will require major surgery before they even begin to function properly again. This will make them unwilling to have another go unless they're thoroughly prepared. Before you set somebody up, go over the whole process in your mind before you do it. If you've worked out people's agendas, you'll know roughly where each person will stand and how they will react in a given situation. Be prepared for all consequences and have your lines ready.

Avoiding the ambush

The whole point of an ambush is the element of surprise. When pushed or threatened, some people can become very nasty, little aliens in fact, who lurk in dark corners and then jump on somebody's face. If you find you can't see the light at the end of the tunnel and you're having trouble breathing, then you've probably got an alien on your face.

If you've been successfully ambushed, there are some things you can do to recover, including going over their head and getting advice from outside authorities, but there are many things you can do to avoid an ambush. Once the element of surprise is lost, then you can smile secretly to yourself as you watch the action unfolding, secure in the knowledge that they are about to set themselves up.

The diary

The diary is one of the most useful tools you can use to get somebody while simultaneously protecting yourself. It may be useful to add that diary notes can be used as evidence in a court of law. Get yourself a nice big diary (if the company won't give you one, buy one yourself) and write in it not only all your appointments and tasks, but also verbal requests. Note down the time and a shorthand version of what occurred. This is particularly useful when bosses ask you to do something and then forget to tell you that they actually don't want you to do it. Write down all requests from anybody who may want to have a go at you and from anybody senior to you. This is to prevent the senior person from turning around and blaming you. Naturally, any company worth anything at all is not going to take this kind of rubbish from management — the reason why they are managers is because they take responsibility for things — but some companies just do not know the meaning of professionalism.

Human nature — letting the boss know they're the boss

As we've already stated, you should never win an argument with your boss. You must always give them the respect they deserve for being the boss. Even if they are wrong, making a fool of them publicly by pointing this out will make them determined to bury you. Nobody likes being backed into a corner. Once backed into the corner, they will win any dispute. They have more power and more friends in high places and you are only a mere minion. You've got to give them plenty of room to move and retain their dignity, pride and self-respect. If they concede that you may be correct, they've got to look as if they thought of it. Here's an example of a way of getting out of a sticky situation, and a way to get permanently stuck in it.

Your boss has just designed a promotional campaign for your company, which manufactures, among other things, hot-air balloons. The campaign, which is to run in all the major national media, features a giant hot-air balloon floating lazily in the cloud-specked sky and has the line: 'We'll take you to places you've never been'. So far, so good. At first glance anybody looking at it would think 'What fun! Doesn't it look dreamy?' But you know from the newspapers, unlike your boss who reads the newspapers on an ad hoc basis, that in the past few months there have been three hot-air balloon accidents in which people plunged to their deaths. Consequently, you think it would be a very bad idea to run a campaign along these lines at this time.

'Yeah, we'll take you to a place you've never been: your funeral' you think to yourself, as you look at this glossy suicide campaign. Somehow, it's got to be stopped, even though your boss treats you like a complete fool and listens to nothing you say, and the campaign is in the final proof stage before being sent to the ad agency.

The wrong way

You: **'This is ridiculous, this campaign. We are going to look like heartless murderers!'**
Your boss: 'What do you mean?'

You: **'Don't you know there have been some hot-air balloon accidents in the past few months? People were killed!'**
Your boss: 'I didn't know. I haven't had time to read all the papers lately.'

You: **'Well, there have been three accidents, up North. About five people have died, I think.'**
Your boss: 'Well, I don't see that it makes any difference. It was a few months ago, now.'

You: **'But it will make a difference! We've got to stop it!'**
Your boss: 'You're way out of line here. I know what's going

on and I can assure you that nobody will even notice. We're running with it. Thank you for your comments but I think I know a bit more about the market than you do. I have been here for 15 years, after all.'

The right way

Take your boss right out of the picture. Go to the next person in senior management who likes you but doesn't really like your boss, who has his/her eye on your boss's job, and is looking for an opportunity to have a go. In this you play the role of agent provocateur. You set them up, but nobody knows it was you — the work equivalent of shouting 'Fire!' in a crowded theatre. ('Who shouted that?' 'I don't know, I couldn't see them! Let's just run for the exits!')

You: **'Hi, do you have a minute?'**
Other manager: 'Yeah, sure. How can I help you?'

You: **'Well, I was just looking at this ad that my boss is running.'**
Other manager: 'Yes? Well, it looks all right to me.'

You: **'Oh, it's a great concept, no doubt about that. It's just that I had a feeling there may be some backlash from this given that there have been some hot-air balloon accidents in the last few months.'**
Other manager: 'Mmmm. I knew there was one. But have there been more? I wish I'd seen this before, then I would have picked it up long ago. What does your boss say about it?'

You: **'Well, he's very busy, as you know, and I guess he hasn't had much time to catch up on current affairs. I don't think he knows about it. I'm just very concerned, for the company's reputation.'**
Other manager: 'Why don't you have a word to him?'

You: **'He's very tired today, he's been working very long hours. He tends to snap at me when I bother him.'**
Other manager: 'Yes, well, I'll have a word to him, if you like.'

You: **'Oh, would you? I'd appreciate it.'**
Other manager: 'All right. I'll speak to him this afternoon. And thank you for your concern. It won't be forgotten.'

True Crimes — Real Life Story

Susan, 31, was working as a television journalist in one of Australia's more parochial capital cities. Susan was working on an evening current affairs show which prides itself on carrying a large amount of local news. Like every television program, everywhere in the world, the level of paranoia about competing shows on other networks would defy belief to anybody who doesn't work in television. This network, and this program, was no exception to the extent that they considered even the newspapers and radio to be their competitors.

Apart from the national programming, this particular state has several home-grown news efforts on television and radio, one major metropolitan daily newspaper (all of which fight to carry a story of real impact, such as the lowering of speed limits in suburban areas to 40 kilometres an hour), and a widely-read, popular 'alternative' monthly newspaper, which prints critical articles on state politics, local 'celebrities' and lengthy critiques on the arts, which we will call *The Stirrer*, for legal purposes.

For a few months *The Stirrer* had been printing a series of heavily veiled articles criticising the local television media. This made the management at the television station very edgy to begin with. Then *The Stirrer* came right out of the closet and gave a very unflattering review of this program, named people and insisted that the level of journalism displayed on this 'flagship national network' was a disgrace.

The television management were apoplectic with rage. The article had been so full of details, so correct in its assumptions that it was very improbable that the writer of this article had just done his job as a journalist. There had to be a conspiracy and from this they reached the conclusion that there was a spy in their midst.

'They focused on me,' says Susan. 'They called a big meeting on the day *The Stirrer* came out and asked me if I knew who had written it. Of course I did! Even though it was written under a pseudonym, everybody in journalism knows everybody else, particularly in such a small city. In fact, the guy who had written it had asked me to read it over to see that it was factually correct. I didn't have time to do that, so I didn't see it before it went to print — but I agreed absolutely with everything it said.

'Well, you should have seen them. Everybody was shooed out of the office and they sat me there and grilled me for an hour or so. They wanted to know who had written that article and they weren't going to leave me alone until I told them. I'm surprised they didn't get the 100-watt globe out and shine it in my face and stick bamboo shoots up my fingernails. Naturally, I wouldn't tell them. It's against my ethics to do that.

'I was very distressed by this, as it had never happened to me before. They were overreacting in a major way. Then they got nastier and nastier. They threatened a male friend of mine at the time, over lunch, and said that if he continued talking to me his career would be shortened considerably. Anybody who came near me, they harassed. They wouldn't give me any good stories — they were ringing me at home, threatening me with the sack. It was awful. I think it went on for about two months. Their behaviour was consistent with the small-mindedness which the wretched article was criticising them for in the first place! Still, I wouldn't tell them. It's like anything: the more you get pushed the more you hang on to the thing they want. Not that I would have told them anyway, as it's against my principles.

'I was in a bad way. Wasn't eating, wasn't sleeping. I was a pariah. Eventually, there was an ugly scene where I was released from my contract. I have since been unable to work in that particular television network again, and have had to work on more commercial networks. Some of these people have moved subsequently to the bigger, coastal cities and are no doubt using the same tactics on hapless journalists there. I'll never forget those people and what they did — and I am waiting for my revenge because you can't treat people like shit and get away with it.'

Susan's story is a clear case of a network of people who think the same, operating in a way in which a Mafioso would find heartening. There is little one can do about this kind of harassment if all of management are united against you except, possibly, plant a mine or take legal action.

Susan decided not to take legal action, although her friend did. He won his case, but has never worked in the television industry again. Since this episode, Susan has done a number of different things and is now happily enjoying a new career in acting and professional writing.

GOING OVER THEIR HEADS
The roller-coaster ride of anxiety and despair begins for two reasons only: you don't fit in, or you are an unfortunate obstacle in the way of somebody's upward climb. It is not

usually the MD who initiates this process (you know this, because you're still there; MDs ambush people), it's usually somebody who feels threatened by you, or with whom you disagree, who is either on the same level as you or just above you. Either way they want to get rid of you and they will make sure this happens through a nasty and vicious process known as 'wearing you down'. (It is rare that people are sacked because they are incompetent, usually they are moved sideways.) This process means that you will be watched, 'spoken to' weekly, if not daily, and every task given to you will be done on paper, with, possibly, an unachievable deadline attached. During this process, you are alone. Totally alone and you can trust nobody. Everybody, as we have previously mentioned, has their own little agenda and saving you may not be part of their agenda. What you need to do in these situations is not panic, and to keep your head. Now is not a good time to take holidays. Many people have done this to discover, to their horror, that their job has been advertised while they are away.

You will know you've been targeted when you receive the first warning. The first warning does not constitute a verbal dressing-down but is a written precis of exactly what you are doing wrong and how it can be fixed. In the public service, a person must receive three of these memos, along with counselling and plenty of room for restitution, before any action can be taken. In the private sector, it is becoming more and more difficult to sack people who are incompetent as the rules are tightening up. They have to have very good reasons for sacking you and they have to prove that you are so incompetent that you are a liability to the company, rather than an asset. Then, there will be less danger of you taking them to court for wrongful dismissal.

However, people have been known to recover at various stages of the wearing-down process, which happen in the following phases:

The warning memo

This is the first and, possibly, only chance you will get to make amends. This is the time to take immediate action. When you receive the warning memo, or anything that could be interpreted as a warning memo, read it carefully. Then, work out a response to each charge laid against you and arrange a meeting with the person sending the memo. You then have to decide if this disgusting piece of paper is just a storm in a teacup or likely to be the first stage in a long and ultimately stressful process. With the former, send a memo in response, coupled with a verbal discussion. This ensures that both documents remain on your personnel file, but no further action is taken. With the latter, you're going to have to have another meeting, which you arrange after you've called and met with your union.

The meeting

The aim here is to argue each of these points and achieve something that puts the blame equally on the person receiving the memo and the person sending the memo. It may be necessary to have a third party involved in this meeting for adjudication to prevent ugly scenes along the lines of the 'You did'/'Didn't'/'You did'/'Didn't' circular discussion, poking out of tongues and grabbing people by their collar and spitting on them. In particularly bad situations, you may require an independent observer to take minutes. (Anybody involved in the dispute in any way does not qualify as an independent observer; it is usually the MD's secretary.) Minutes are taken so that if the case ends up going to court (which we don't want) then there is no doubt about what anybody said and what was decided. Of course, it may be in your interests to have no independent observer to take minutes: if the MD is part of the discussion and takes minutes, the court may decide that the MD, as the chief representative of the company you have taken to court, does not qualify as 'independent', and they may throw the case out.

Everybody should be aware of who is going to attend this meeting. If you are ambushed, by more people being there than there should be, for instance, you are quite within your rights to stop the meeting. You do this by saying: 'I'm sorry, I wasn't quite prepared for this situation. I'm afraid we're going to have to schedule the meeting for another time.' They can't make you take part in a meeting of this nature. And your entrance and spectacular exit, along with what you said, have to be minuted. You can do the same thing if you feel that you just can't manage any longer and are either going to grab the MD by his tie and choke him until his face turns purple, or burst into tears. Remember, also, that you do not have to answer all the questions just because they are asked of you. You can say: 'I'm sorry, I'm not really in a position to answer that question at this time'. This is not a court of law and you are under no obligation whatsoever except the obligation of resolving the issue at hand.

The second warning memo

If the prior situation was resolved, then there should be no second warning memo. If there is, they're definitely out to get you and step one has to be endured all over again. You might want to start looking around the traps for another job, just to be on the safe side.

The third warning memo

Hope you're looking for another job. If you've been offered one, take it.

Taking legal action

If you feel that you have been unfairly dismissed, professionally harassed or victimised then you can take some kind of action. One really should call one's union before the first meeting takes place. This is for your protection only. Arrange a meeting with them (you'll have to invent a death or doctor's appointment as all eyes will be upon you) and discuss your problem. Take all relevant bits of paper. Your union will then give you all sorts of useful advice as to what is the best way to proceed. They may also tell you if there have been any other incidents of the same nature. If there have been, you will get a very good idea of how the company proceeds in these situations and what they are likely to do to you.

Never tell them directly that you are going to see your union. A freak-out will be the minimal response if they find out this is happening. What you need to do is imply or leak the fact that you are 'seeking legal advice'. This will be enough for them to pull back a bit. If they sack you after you've been to see the union, they will probably have to endure a long and expensive court case, whereas if they sack you before you see them, you won't have much of a leg to stand on. The trick here is to prevent them from taking advantage of this Window of Opportunity. Speak to nobody. Keep it to yourself and stay one step ahead of them.

The mere thought of union involvement gives even the most mild-mannered company director heart palpitations. At this early stage, it's best to keep it as a threat. Full-blown union involvement, no matter how conciliation-oriented, will make people think you are a litigious troublemaker and can make it terribly difficult for you to work in the same industry again, particularly if it's a small one. Although it is illegal for people not to be employed because they've been involved in some dispute, this is very hard to prove. People talk over the phone, at dinner parties, at the local shop. Information gets around in a small or closed industry and soon you'll find you can't work in the industry again.

True Crimes — Real Life Story

'I inherited a bunch of conspiracy theorists when I was promoted,' says Robert, administration manager for a company that manufactures burglar alarms. 'These were the kind of people convinced not only that there was a conspiracy to assassinate JFK, but that Elvis is still alive and there really are the bodies of aliens hidden somewhere in the United States. You know the type, don't you?'

Recently elevated to management, Robert found he was working long hours trying to pull his team together getting them to achieve on time all the things his division was responsible for, including the pays and the entire accounting system. His team consisted of five data processors — four women and one man. He found he had no trouble with the lone male but the women were a real problem.

'They had a female boss before me who, quite frankly, was very good at her job but was a complete bitch,' he says. 'She was a stickler for equal opportunity and was always saying the company was sexist without taking into account the personalities of those involved in these incidents.

'This pack of women did everything together: they drove each other to work, they had lunch together, they saw each other on the weekend. There was something wrong with each of them: not major personality disorders, but neuroticism in general. They fed off each other's problems like a bunch of parasites, egging each other on and whingeing constantly about their problems. They were incredibly negative; it was always somebody else's fault, never their own. It was always because they were women, or because somebody had made a pass at one of them which was rejected. (Personally, I think that was a load of hogwash.) I don't think they had much of a life: there were no men in it at all.'

Robert found that these women viewed him with contempt through eyes slanty with suspicion and blocked everything he initiated or changed. They did this by covering up each other's mistakes, lying for each other and doing everything incredibly slowly. Robert had to break this charmed circle and did this by picking the ringleader and engaging in the wearing-down process.

'There was no doubt that Rhonda was the ringleader,' continues Robert.

'She had major problems with men — she'd suffered a very bitter divorce and could no longer play Lady Bountiful and the Beloved Wife, flashing huge great diamond rings and bragging about her holiday to Bali. Suddenly, she was nobody. She hated men and particularly, me. I think maybe I reminded her of her husband in some way. She had major attitude problems, was dreadfully unhappy and was more of a hindrance than a help.'

Robert decided that if Rhonda could be brought into line, the others would follow. He did this by watching her every second of the day.

'It was a major hassle for me,' he says. 'My job description had changed from administration manager to Rhonda monitor. I watched everything she did. If she arrived at work ten minutes late, I noted it down. If she took longer than 45 minutes for lunch I wrote it down. If she left early without asking, that went in the book too. I would lurk in the warehouse, pretending to be counting stock, while I eyeballed Rhonda from between piles of crates, gossiping. I would wait five minutes and then nonchalantly wander out, asking her about some project that hadn't been finished. It got to the point where, whenever I approached her, even her hair clenched up.

'She thought she was safe, foolish woman, because she believed she was more powerful than she was but her umbrella of protection (her former boss) had left. She got the first warning memo, and the second. Her life was a living hell and so was mine — I was there until ten or 11 at night catching up on all the work I should have done during the day when I was watching Rhonda.

'Finally, she left. She just couldn't take it anymore. The others quickly came into line when they saw what happened. They didn't want to be shoved out into the cold with a mortgage to pay off and three kids to look after. The whole process took about eight months, but I don't regret one moment of it.'

GET YOUR MONKEY OFF MY BACK

Monkeys are little problems or tasks that are not your responsibility and that you do not want to take on. You've got enough monkeys of your own without having anybody else's. Monkeys are apt to jump onto your back in your first few months at the company. This is why you need to have a job description so that you know exactly what you are supposed to do.

If somebody comes up to you and asks you to do something for them 'as a favour' as they are sooooo busy, think carefully before you take it on. It may be the kind of thing that grows and grows like Pinocchio's nose. If it is a small thing, like photocopying something, then you can probably do it. But watch out that you don't give people the impression that you'll do something for them every time they ask. My recommendation would be to do nothing for anybody else until you know exactly what your own job is.

You can stop this kind of behaviour by saying: 'I'm sorry, I'd love to help, but I can't do anything at the moment until I've done all this work my boss just gave me', or 'I'll have to check with my supervisor — I have to run everything through him/her'. If you've just taken on a management position watch out for your 'team members' coming to you with every single little problem they have. Insignificant things like where to move a bookcase should not require wide consultation of managers.

True Crimes — Real Life Story

'There is a very good Hitchcock film called *The Trouble With Harry*,' begins Antoinette, crossing her legs while leaning confidentially forward. 'I worked with a Harry once. In the film, the trouble with Harry was that he was dead and everybody had a hell of a time trying to hide the body. The problem with my Harry was that he didn't realise he was the problem.

'His problem was that anybody who wore a skirt automatically became relegated to the level of secretary. I knew there was something wrong with him when he said that his secretary was "incompetent". I remember being astounded at this, and saying to him: "Well, if she's so incompetent why is she still working for you?". I mean, he hired her.

'One day, the poor "incompetent" secretary wasn't there and every other woman in the place must have shot off as soon as they realised what was going to happen. But not me, of course, because I made the presumption that because I was a manager (the only woman in management by the way) he wouldn't approach me.

'Imagine my surprise when I looked up from my desk and saw a shape that gradually materialised into that of Harry. He was holding a pile of papers and dribbling on about "helping" him with something. It quickly transpired that what he was trying to do was flatter me into doing his typing for him!

'I was so surprised that I said the first thing that came into my head, which was "Look, I'm sorry but I'm not a secretary. Can't you get somebody else to do it for you?" and he replied venomously: "I can't believe you're not going to help me. I'll have a few words to say about your unhelpful attitude" and stalked off.

'I didn't think anything of it until I received an internal phone call and an unidentified male voice said: "Well done, Antoinette, well done!" and there was a definite note of jubilation in his voice. I thought that was fairly strange but I wasn't worried because my boss, a wonderful American and recent import, had very clear ideas about this sort of behaviour.

'It transpired that Harry had walked into Mark's office (the boss) and had loudly proclaimed on my "unhelpfulness" and general "bad attitude". Mark had turned around and asked him exactly what he wanted help with. Harry had indicated vaguely this pile of papers (which he was still clutching to his bosom by the way). Mark had to wrestle them out of his grip. And then he had uttered these joyous words: "I pay Antoinette to fulfil her position as a manager of this company, not to do your typing. You can do your own typing."

'From that day forward Harry did not utter another syllable to my face. Which was a good thing, really, as that made him almost as good as dead.'

DELEGATION — PASSING ON THE DOOMED PET PROJECT

There is usually one project floating around every office which never seems to get finished. The reason is because it's a useless idea. The project is usually the brainchild of the managing director or somebody in senior management who doesn't really know what they are doing. Nobody wants to have anything to do with it as the thing stinks like a three-day-old corpse and is going to imbue the person who works on it with the stench of death.

If you've got stuck with this sucker you've got to get rid of it. For a start it's a bad idea, but it also means that you are going to have a lot more interaction with the managing director than is good for your, or his/her health. Nobody wants to be right under the eye of the teacher all the time. Things might be noticed that do not redound to your credit.

If you get it, you've got to keep putting it right at the bottom of your list of projects. In this, you've got to tacitly enlist the support of your immediate boss, who will want his/her special projects finished before this big fat stinker anyway. You've got to keep saying that your list of priorities means that you do not have enough time to do nearly as much on this project as you would like to. You then, cleverly, wait for it to be suggested that perhaps somebody could work on it with you. The trick here is to enlist as many people as possible to help with this rotten idea. You wait for your superior to choose who is lucky enough to work on it with you. (This is very similar to a military commander saying: 'I need three volunteers to go up over that hill and see how many Indians there are.' There is a deathly silence. 'OK. You, you and you,' he says, pointing at three unfortunates. 'Thank you for volunteering.') Once you've got somebody else involved, you can gradually and surreptitiously hand more and more bits of it over until you have offloaded responsibility for the whole thing.

AVOIDING THE BOOMERANG EFFECT

It's amazing how, as old grudges come up in arguments with your partner ('This is just like that time at your mother's house when you didn't support me!' which gets the response 'What time are you talking about?' in a frustrated tone. 'You know, Barbara's birthday when I made that strawberry cheesecake and your mother said I couldn't cook!' followed by 'That was 13 years ago for Christ's sake! That's ridiculous!'), old projects and mistakes have a tendency to come back with the speed of a boomerang and hit you in the back of the neck.

You think it's over, but it isn't. A boomerang can be some horrible old project that you thought, mistakenly, that somebody else was handling. You discover that that wasn't their impression of the situation at all, and that you are still responsible. Or it can be an ancient stuff-up from a few years back that everyone remembers vividly and refers to in any performance review where somebody wants to get you, implying a history of behaviour along these lines.

You can avoid the boomerang by:
◎ Keeping communication lines open
◎ Giving project delegation in written form

- Being consistent in your professional behaviour
- Making as few stuff-ups as possible
- Covering up those you make as best you can
- Making sure all issues are fully resolved before proceeding
- Making sure that everyone realises there are two sides to every story
- Constantly reiterating who is responsible in written or verbal form

PHRASES THAT WILL GET YOU OUT OF TROUBLE — MORE WORKSPEAK

Language is one of the most important tools you have at your disposal in the workplace. A couple of tips: never say what you're really thinking and always use touchy-feely terms: 'I feel' instead of 'I think', and 'Perhaps we should'... instead of 'What we should do is ...'. Here are some primary examples of Workspeak 'FYI' (for your information).

'That's an interesting point of view.'
Actual meaning: It's not very interesting at all and is, in fact, a ludicrous point of view but you are too polite to say so.

'Yes, I do see what you mean.'
Actual meaning: You do. You just don't agree with it.

'That's understandable.'
Actual meaning: You know why they did it, but you would never have done it yourself.

'I wish I'd said that.'
Actual meaning: You're glad you didn't.

'They have an unfortunate manner.'
Actual meaning: They are complete and utter bastards/bitches.

'They're unique.'
Actual meaning: They're completely psychotic and should be committed, instantly.

'You obviously know what you're doing.'
Actual meaning: You don't think they do, but who are you going to tell?

'There must have been a communication problem.'
Actual meanings:
a. There wasn't. You're just letting them off the hook.
b. You stuffed up but you're not going to tell them that.

'That's an unusual idea. Perhaps we should discuss it with my superior.'
Actual meaning: It's a stupid idea, and your superior will agree with you.

'Yes, but they've had a lot of personal problems.'
Actual meaning: They're unstable and not to be trusted with any responsibility whatsoever.

'X is so good at what she does. She is really very capable. I'm sure with a bit of nurturing she would really blossom.'
Actual meaning: You don't want to do it, and you're trying to unload it onto somebody else while appearing encouraging.

'We're always open to suggestions.'
Actual meaning: You're not. It just makes them think they've contributed.

'I would prefer it if you did this'
Actual meaning: Do it my way.

'I feel there may be some crossed wires.'
Actual meaning: We don't understand each other. You're too stupid.

'Do you have a problem with that?'
Actual meaning: I don't care if you do. We're doing it this way.

QUESTIONS YOU SHOULD NEVER ANSWER HONESTLY

- 'So, how are you finding the job?'
- 'What do you think of my haircut?'
- 'What happened in the meeting?'
- 'What do you think of Robert/Amanda?'
- 'What are you doing on the weekend?'
- 'Are you coming over for the staff Christmas barbeque?'
- 'Do you think Richard really knows what he's doing?'
- 'What is your company's turnover?'
- 'How much do you earn?'
- 'What do you think of group sex?'
- 'Are you gay/a lesbian?'
- 'How old are you?'
- 'Where do you see yourself in five years time?'
- 'What are your weakest qualities in a work situation?'
- 'Ever been sacked or involved in a union dispute?'
- 'Have you read *American Psycho*?'

QUESTIONS YOU SHOULD ALWAYS ANSWER HONESTLY

- 'Are you going to get the project in on time?'
- 'Are you having any problems?'
- 'Is there anything I can help you with?'
- 'Do you think I should leave the company?'
- 'Do you want to go to lunch?' (The answer is always 'yes' if it's your boss.)
- 'Would you like to come and have dinner with my family?' (As above.)
- 'Would you like a pay rise?'
- 'What are your greatest strengths in a work situation?'
- 'Would you like a company car?'

- 'Do you want to go to America for our sales conference?'
- 'Do you want to come to my church and speak in tongues next Saturday?'
- 'I really believe Elvis is still alive. What do you think?'

FOOT-IN-MOUTH DISEASE

These are the things you should never, ever answer, ask or say. Put a couple of drinks into most people and not only do they start telling you about their sordid and pathetic sex life, but they also say all the things that people are thinking secretly but would never dare say in the cold, sober light of day. Here are some prime examples:

- 'Is that a toupee?'
- 'Are you pregnant?'
- 'I hate Newtown. Full of bloody poofters and those bloody ugly women wearing boiler suits. Bloody horrible place.'
- 'Let's be honest — all she really needs is a good f—k. Not that she's got much chance of getting one, I reckon.'
- 'You've put on a bit of weight, haven't you?'
- 'I tell you, this company would be stuffed if it wasn't for me. You've got no idea of the amount of work I do. The number of times I've saved this company from ruin, you just wouldn't believe . . . '
- 'I reckon Kim Beazley was a used-car salesman in a previous life, and as for that Johnny Howard, wouldn't trust him as far as I could throw him. I always say, "Never trust a man who looks like he's standing in a trench".' (Don't say things like this: you just never know where Labor-ites or Liberal-ites are hiding.)
- 'Why don't you just sack the stupid bastard?'
- 'He's a stupid, incompetent, bloody black fool!' (Goes down really well in the public service.)

- 'Did you hear the one about ... ?' (Jokes about dead babies, animals, disabled people, terminal disease and race are not a good idea. Apart from the fact that they are in incredibly bad taste, you never know if the person you're working with thinks that even vegetables have souls and won't take kindly to your rude comments on this issue, particularly if she's the boss. Say what you want at your own dinner-table but not at work.)
- 'You can trust me absolutely, you know. Absolutely.'
- 'Don't tell anybody, but ...'

Resignation, dismissal or retrenchment

Network chief after retrenching employee: 'Now, if there's anything I can do for you...'

Employee: 'Well, I certainly hope you'll die soon.' BROADCAST NEWS

RECOGNISING THE DANGER SIGNALS OF AN IMMINENT SACKING

There comes a time in all working lives, when your time is up. It is not usually of your own volition but it is sometimes better to leave than to continue to grind away under the illusion that your career might actually be going somewhere. You've got to make sure, whether you've resigned or been retrenched, that you salvage as much as possible from the situation by reading the section 'Getting the sack' and followed by 'Recognising the danger signals'. If any of the following happen to you, then start looking seriously in the employment section. Start panicking when:

◎ You are given multiple projects. This is usually done with the statement: 'You're a truly valued member of the team

and you've been producing such high-quality work that we have absolute faith in your ability to manage it'.
- Along with this, you are given impossible deadlines.
- You are given two minutes notice of important meetings.
- You find that nobody will have lunch with you.
- You're seeing the MD more than you should — and it's not socially.
- You are asked to hand in weekly, written reports.
- Sorting through your in-tray becomes critical to your day-to-day functioning.
- Colleagues surreptitiously say 'You might find this useful' while throwing a confidential memo onto your desk.
- You are given the 'attitude speech'. This is the speech where management cannot fault your work in any way and so decide that you have a bad attitude. Of course, by this stage you probably do.
- All information is committed to memory.
- You feel compelled to take copies of everything and hide them in your file at home.
- You've been nursing a concept from embryo stage and two days prior to it hatching it's taken away from you.
- Your boss comes into your office at 5.00 pm on a Friday with an envelope in hand.

True Crimes — Real Life Story

Alex had been looking forward to his holiday. He hadn't had one for a few years, being more concerned with building up his reputation in the company. He imagined a wide stretch of beach, unending sunshine and silver trays bearing a variety of spectacular drinks decorated with pieces of fruit and festive umbrellas.

He did not know exactly when this holiday was going to materialise but he was determined to have one and spent a lot of his time thinking about it. He had an idea he wanted to go somewhere tropical and even purchased a series of shirts which would amaze and astonish the local inhabitants with their magnificence.

But the winds of change were blowing in Alex's direction in the form of a new member of the 'team', on the same level as Alex in a closely related division — a smart and sassy person from overseas who was bright and bubbly and full of new ideas. The managing director (herself from overseas) took a shine to her and Alex found himself, after years of considerable hard work, on the outer.

'The woman was a whirling dervish,' he says. 'Within weeks of her arrival we were being showered with innovation, at the express invitation of the managing director, and I was being pushed and pummelled and squeezed and cajoled into supporting every single one of this woman's ideas, even though I didn't agree with a lot of them.

'But what could I do?' he continues. 'She had the support of the Powers That Be. Initially I did the best I could to divert her from projects I thought totally silly and to put an absolute stop to some that would have been nothing but disasters. Even though she was always polite to me, I somehow felt wary of her. I had a feeling she had her eye on my division. In fact, she had mentioned, in an offhand, jokey manner, that it would be "a great idea for the divisions to combine under one manager", followed by ominous words like "profitability" and "efficiency".'

The wind started blowing a little harder when, becoming a little anxious about the situation, Alex started to really dig his heels in. It became a state of civilised, rigid cold war with Alex creating as many obstacles as he could. But he still talked about his holiday. He was so tired and worried that he felt a bit of a break would do him good. And where on earth would he be able to wear all those really quite unusual shirts if not on his planned holiday? With no real sense of misgiving he finalised his travel arrangements, ignoring the long meeting with the managing director about his 'attitude problem' and his 'inability to work in a team'. He ignored the large pile of memos on his desk on his last day before he boarded the plane to rest and relaxation — didn't even glance at them. They could wait until he got back.

The ill-wind had turned into a hurricane when Alex, lying replete in his deckchair, opened the 'Employment' section of the metropolitan newspaper and found to his horror that his job had been advertised. 'A new division of the company has been created, with an opening for an assistant to the manager. Please send your résumé to...' and there was the name of the bright, sassy 'team player'.

And the moral of this story is: when you feel that the times they are a changing, *never* go on holiday.

RESIGNATION LETTERS

Once you've decided to take a step towards a better life there is a good way of doing it and a bad way of doing it.

Here is an example of a bad resignation letter:

28 November   Your address
To: The Managing Director
(Yippee!)

Dear John,
I wish to tender my resignation effective week ending 8 December (next week). I can't convey to you how happy this

decision has made me. It makes me feel good to know that I won't have to put up with your ugly faces and your idiotic work practices that masquerade as professional behaviour.

You're all a big, fat joke!

See you later, suckers,

Signed by You (in blue crayon)

We all know that this is really what you want to say, but what you've got to do is convey how annoyed you are and how useless you think they are without actually being absolutely direct about it. You can even name people, depending on how you do it.

Here are two versions of the perfect resignation letter:

28 September   Your address
Acme Products
31 Castle Grove
To: The Managing Director

Dear John,
It is with regret that I resign from the position as Advertising Manager with Acme Products effective Friday 9 December.

This step has been taken due to the continuing lack of communication and organisation within the Advertising Department. Issues that were raised in May by me, regarding concerns with Roger Forwood and the department, have not been addressed or changed: no improvement has been noticeable. Neither has any effort been made on the part of senior management to ensure issues raised at that time have been resolved.

As there has been no change in Roger Forwood's professional approach, I am left with no choice but to resign, six months after I first joined the company.

I very much enjoyed the challenges of working with clients of such high quality and international recognition and I am sorry that my skills and qualifications could not have been used to assist Acme Products' development in the future. I was particularly pleased to work with Deborah de Angelis, and especially lucky to work with Roger Mainwaring, from whose knowledge and professionalism I greatly benefited.

I wish Acme Products every success with their future projects and development.

Yours sincerely,
Signed by You (in pen)

What follows is a toned-down version of the previous letter:

28 September   Your address
Acme Products
31 Castle Grove
Attention: The Managing Director

Dear John,
It is with regret that I wish to formally tender my resignation from my position at Acme Products and thereby advise you of the required notice: one week.

I have become increasingly aware that my current position cannot offer me the latitude of experience, involvement and indeed fulfilment that I had hoped for. Ultimately, in the interest of my professional career development I am pursuing a different aspect of the industry.

Thank you for the opportunity of working with Acme Products.

Yours sincerely,
Signed by You (in pen)

THE BRONZE HANDSHAKE: RETRENCHMENT AND REDUNDANCY

Although a sorry event, retrenchment can sometimes be a better alternative to resignation, and is definitely preferable to getting the sack. At least you get the opportunity to explain the sudden end of your job reasonably and believably. Retrenchment may also provide you with funds (depending on your length of service) to pursue a special endeavour or keep the roof over your head while you look for another job. However, if you feel your 'retrenchment' was a blind for 'sacking without any reason' (particularly if you see your exact position advertised), you may want to contact your union for advice. But remember that if this is the scenario, then it was probably only a matter of time before they forced you into resigning anyway.

Think carefully before you accept a voluntary redundancy package, particularly if you want to start your own business with the money. The less visible benefits of full-time employment — annual leave, sick leave, long service leave and superannuation — can often be overlooked. Add to that the statistics that more than 50 per cent of small businesses fail in the first two years and 74 per cent of small businesses employ less than five people, and you'll realise that it's a good idea to prepare for your retrenchment or redundancy exactly as if you were resigning. The following sections will give you some tips.

MAKING THE MOST OF YOUR EXIT INTERVIEW

This is your big opportunity to say all the things you want to say, even if they don't ask you. Your resignation should be tendered to the most senior person in the company, who will listen to everything you have to say. Getting a few words in the MD's shell-like ear is worthwhile. This is the only situation when you should answer all the questions honestly. Really professional companies hold exit interviews because they are smart enough to realise that your debriefing, and the manner in which you leave the company, are just as important as how you joined it.

Getting the big picture is what MDs are all about and your comments, ascerbic or otherwise, will help to illuminate it. Always start off by thanking them for the opportunity to work with them and then wait for the questions to roll. Using Workspeak, you should be able to nail a few people in the nicest possible way, or at the very least, lay a few mines to be stepped on in the future.

Following this gratifying interview, you will be given some kind of exit party to mark the occasion. (If you have resigned on the same day or have been sacked with several ugly scenes still vivid in collective memory, you will not have to endure this hypocritical sadness at your parting. In this case, you will have been, probably, divested of your keys, car and security number, and escorted to the door, where a taxi sits waiting.)

The exit party is usually drinks after work, where you have to go around and say how much you enjoyed working with everybody and how sad you are at having to leave. At some point, somebody will have a few kind words to say and you can then make a speech in return. This is another big opportunity to single out those who have helped you (name them) and those who have hindered you (omit them). If your boss has been your sole reason for leaving, don't mention him in your speech. Ignore him completely. Somebody I knew omitted her boss in her speech, but then gave him some very beautiful crystal glasses 'to fill up with Scotch, which you'll be needing' she said as she handed the gift-wrapped package over. He was suddenly put on the spot and looked highly embarrassed (needless to say he hadn't bought her anything) and looked like the cheap, lousy manager he actually was, while she looked like a terribly nice person who had been victimised (which is exactly what had happened). She made the point with subtlety and style.

GETTING RID OF INCRIMINATING EVIDENCE

If you've resigned or been retrenched you've probably been cleaning up after yourself, photocopying bits of paper and smuggling them home. If you've been sacked, and you have to leave immediately, then you'd better hope you didn't leave those threatening letters written in cat's blood which say: 'I know where you live' in your top drawer, or the yearly subscription to *Hootin' Hooters!* magazine.

Before you leave, go through all your computer files and trash anything that may incriminate you at a later date. If you're not sure what to do with it, trash it anyway. Leave them only with plain facts that the next poor person who's doing the job can use.(However, be warned — even though you have trashed your files from your hard disk, they can still be retrieved if someone is really desperate to find out what you were up to in your last weeks with the company.)

Take everything that belongs to you with you — particularly your contacts. After all, the next person who's doing the job should have their own contacts. Just like renting a flat, you want to leave the place exactly as you found it, spick, span and sparse.

You want to make your exit as bloodless as you can. Don't reveal your contempt for or animosity toward those who have done you wrong. That will only make them more likely to give a negative report of you over the phone to one of their mates when you are applying for the next job.

REFERENCES

Get as many written references as you possibly can when you leave a company. Glowing references do not usually come with dismissal, which is why it's better to resign voluntarily. Choose your referees carefully to ensure that they will say just as many nice things over the phone about you as they will on paper. If you can't get a reference from your company, ask your friends to exaggerate their current jobs and write them for you. If nobody will do anything at all for you, take a stack of company letterhead home and write references yourself using the names of people who have left the company, and can't be traced.

Getting over it and getting on with it

ten

'What about a talk-show host? I think I'd be good at that. I talk to people all the time. How do you get that though?' *FINDING A NEW CAREER FOR GEORGE*, SEINFELD

WORK IS NOT YOUR LIFE

Contrary to popular belief, work is not your life. You work *for* a life: not instead of one. You will meet many people in the working world, many of whom do not have a life. You will meet some people (most of whom are described in the section on 'Identifying alien types') and you will think to yourself 'I wonder what they do when they're not working?'. The answer, of course, is that they don't do anything at all. Work is all they do.

They're easy to spot, your work colleagues who do not have a life. They're the ones who are still there at 8.00 pm and, usually, they're not working but having a few drinks in the boss's office. They're there because that's where the bar fridge is — and the boss is the one with the key. The bosses who don't have a life are also easy to spot. At 5.30 pm on the dot, they're waving their poor harassed employees into their office, encouraging them to 'have a gin and tonic, a beer, whatever you want'. They encourage you to eat chips and other substances masquerading as food. Before you know it, they're engaging in an endless monologue about their broken marriage(s), their children who don't talk to them, or their mother who is now conveniently placed in a rest home. Finally, at 9.00 pm, they say they really should be going home. You suspect that they are going home to the rest of the bottle of Scotch or a cosy night on the couch with the telly for company. And you are right.

Work has a peculiar propensity to eat away at your spare time. And after all, spare time is what you're working *for*, isn't it? If you have other things to do, like family, like friends, like that new play you're in, then you have a good excuse to leave work and not allow your employers to steal your time. These things are just as important as, if not more important than, work. Saying to your boss: 'I can't stay for drinks tonight as I want to spend some time with my husband, wife, lover, family, sister, pet snake, hamster, the man next door, the drunk at the end of the street' is perfectly valid and reasonable, particularly if you have spent the last three weeks having drinks at work. The only reason you're polite about it is because they are paying you money.

WHAT THE HELL AM I DOING HERE?

This is the eternal cry of every human being. Why am I here? Is it really all about the Big Bang or is there Something Else? Does God exist? The job offer has arrived but before you take it and possibly get yourself into another bad situation, it might be a good idea to work out exactly *why* you want it. Feeling compelled to take it is probably not a good enough reason. If you feel that you would probably be better suited to giving critical analyses of Kylie's video clips then, unless that's what you've been offered, you'd better think again.

Fortunately, thinking about why you are working will not drive you as crazy as thinking about the edge of the universe. Most people, except for a fortunate few whom we envy and despise, work for the money. Apart from the obvious financial reasons for working — because you want a house, a car or $200 to spend on your matchbox car collection — there should be a few others. Perhaps you would like to gain more skills so that you can move to a better job with more money, which will enable you to buy $400 worth of matchbox cars every week. Perhaps you would like to work in this particular industry or company because it's a step towards the company you eventually want to work for. Whatever your financial goals, it's a good idea to work out what your other goals may be. Working just for the hell of it is not a good idea.

PHILOSOPHY, MORALS AND ETHICS

These are much maligned in our modern-day world, but it's a good idea to have some. Look at your life and what you believe in. If you really believe that we are polluting the planet, then working in a factory that manufactures styrofoam cups is probably not the best place to be.

It is a well-known fact that we work successfully in what we enjoy and what we believe to be right. Look at your interests: is there an industry or a closely related business sector that you could move into? Work out what your morals and ethics are. If, after much soul-searching, you decide that you don't have any at all, you can look forward to a rewarding career in public relations or advertising.

Working out why you are working is a good first step to deciding what is reasonable to be asked of you and what is not. This is called ethics. It will also be useful to you when you are working out other people's agendas. (See Chapter 4,

'New kid on the block — the basics'.) All jobs challenge people's ideas about the world, and often ask people to do or say things with which they disagree. It may be something as simple as being charming to some fat, sleazy, important overseas company director or something more difficult, like changing the dollar figure on a public report. Either way, you need to know exactly where you stand on various issues. If your company culture doesn't actually require you to lie, but doesn't also insist on you telling the whole truth either (as in advertising or journalism) then be prepared to walk an ethical tightrope on various issues.

True Crimes — Real Life Story

Dianne is a 27-year-old marketing manager working in the entertainment industry. Part of her job means that she is required on occasion to stretch the truth somewhat when copywriting video covers. A ludicrous B-grade copy of Robocop has to be made to sound exciting and action-packed, even if the lead actor is wearing a motorcycle helmet, a joke orange moustache and the quality is such that it sounds like it was filmed in a tin shed in the middle of a hailstorm. However, Dianne decides that, ethically speaking, she can manage this. After all, popular culture being what it is, there will probably be somebody out there who enjoys it. But when she is asked to work on a particularly violent film, she decides to draw the line. The film features a lot of unnecessary blood and gore (the special effects are very well done) hung on a plot thinner than a spider's web. She believes it is violent, immoral and dangerous.

After thinking it over, she decides she will not work on the film and is prepared to take the consequences: losing her job. She discusses the issue with her superior and outlines the reasons why she doesn't want to work on it. Being fully prepared for the door to be opened for her as a prelude to her leaving the office forever, she is pleasantly surprised to find that her superior sees her point of view and gives the film to somebody else to work on. Dianne is given the third in a series of standard action films featuring Sylvester Stallone. It's bad: but it's not that bad.

THE BIG PICTURE — RETAINING PERSPECTIVE

If you want to succeed in anything at all, particularly work, you should try and make it just one part of your life. This will help you to retain a sense of humour and, more importantly, perspective. When you go home livid with rage over the fact that your assistant inveigled you yet again into making him a cup of coffee, you will appreciate the fact that the people you go skydiving with not only do not want to know about your assistant, but do not care. They will laugh and will tell you to forget about it. And they're right. After all, shouldn't you be concentrating on when to pull the ripcord?

RUNNING AWAY MONEY

This is the linchpin to success in your working life. As soon as you get a decent job, start packing some money away. It will be very useful to you if things go horribly wrong which (although we hope and pray this won't happen) they have been known to do on occasion. This is your running away money. It gives you the freedom to decide if you can stand the situation any longer or if you have to free yourself from the chains of bondage right this second. It will pay your rent for you while you are looking for another job. It will enable you to walk into your boss's office, resignation firmly clutched in your hand, and say: 'I don't need this stinking job. You can take your job and you can stuff it! I'm going to the Bahamas to drink banana daiquiris and I won't think of you for one moment while I am doing it!' We naturally do not recommend this kind of resignation (see 'Making the most of your exit interview') except in situations of extremity.

WHY CAN'T YOU LAUGH ABOUT IT?

Just remember: no matter how bad things have got, you're not going to die. Nobody ever died from some fiasco at work. Nobody ever died from making a mistake or losing a job. When you've had a particularly bad day it's true that you may look as if you're dead and yet alive (like Leonard Cohen), but the clammy skin and slow pulse are just signs of fear and guilt — it's not terminal. It's true you may be praying for God to take you early to avoid that ugly scene, but the only thing that's really going to save you is a sense of humour.

True Crimes — Real Life Story

Samantha is a 26-year-old beauty therapist. Her job is tactile: it requires a combination of soothing familiarity and skill. People entrust their bodies to her: they see that face in the mirror every day and they want it to look the best it possibly can. Naturally, the area of the face is a particularly vulnerable one, so imagine Samantha's horror when, in a moment of lapsed concentration, she accidentally waxed off a customer's eyebrow.

'My initial reaction was to vomit,' she said. 'You know you've stuffed up but it's so bad there's nothing you can do about it. There's only two things you can do: go to the pub or vomit.

'I tried not to panic but what can you say? "I'm sorry, I waxed off your eyebrow, I'll draw another one on for you"? I mean, the woman trusted me! So, I just pretended that nothing had gone wrong and I thinned out the other one, to make it look as if it was on purpose. I hovered in front of the mirror as she was leaving, but unfortunately she caught a glimpse of herself in it. Her eyes went wide and there was a sharp intake of breath. But she didn't say anything. It was terrible.

'It took me three days to tell my flatmate about it, I was so ashamed. I had dreams about it. But all my flatmate did was roar with laughter. He thought it was hilarious, and said that it wasn't that bad: "Eyebrows do tend to grow back". I couldn't tell him that sometimes they don't. He told everybody — and they all laughed as well. Maybe, in about ten years time, I'll be able to laugh about it too.'

Even if Samantha didn't amuse herself, she certainly amused a lot of people. Unfortunately, Samantha's Window of Opportunity (the time one has to cover up a mistake) was non-existent. Her only alternatives were to drink a bottle of gin or stand up and face the music. Some comfort can be taken in these situations when you reflect that they are often of the nature commonly known as 'character building'.

TAKING RESPONSIBILITY

This is something that, for some reason, a lot of people are very loath to do. We hear them all the time: 'It wasn't my fault', or 'That happened because so-and-so forgot to do such-and-such'. Once you make a decision, be prepared to defend it — after all, you're the one who made it. If it is quite clear that you made a mistake and your Window of Opportunity no longer exists, then you may as well take responsibility for it. (But as you will see from the section 'Phrases that will get you out of trouble' there are positive ways of saying you made a mistake and negative ways of saying you made a mistake. Don't ever say: 'I made a mistake'. After all, it was only a mistake — we don't want people thinking you're a total incompetent.) If you really believe that something is wrong then say so.

Commenting on the derogatory comment somebody made about somebody else is not going to make you any friends and may even give you the tag of 'troublemaker'. We're talking about important things like sexual harassment, victimisation, or just plain cruelty. Many a person's pain has been relieved because somebody has stood up and been counted.

COMMON SENSE

This is one of the most little-known attributes in today's working world. Before you do anything, anything at all, think about what would be the most sensible way of doing it. Do not let the current corporate culture lure you into thinking that it should be done any other way. Just because it's always been done that way doesn't mean it's the correct way. It's your job and you need to find the fastest, simplest way of doing it so you can concentrate on other, more important, things.

RESPECT

At work, you don't expect people to like you; what you expect them to do is respect you. The first, most basic level of respect should be extended to your work colleagues as fellow human beings. Even if you think someone is a clear-cut case of Invasion of the Body Snatchers, that doesn't excuse rudeness or nastiness. However, the old maxim 'You don't get respect until you've earned it' still holds true. Even if people don't like you they can still respect your professional capabilities, which is why it's important to always be consistent, fair and deliver on time. Business decisions should never be based on how much you like or dislike a person; if you play favourites you're probably going to make the wrong decision.

True Crimes — Real Life Story

'I've come to the conclusion that you can't be friends with the people you work with,' says Samantha, a 32-year-old customer service supervisor. 'When I first started working with the company (a large bank), it was fine.

'We were all in it together, talking to annoyed customers every day. As you can imagine there was a strong sense of camaraderie because nobody likes to be told they're stupid idiots all the time, by people they don't even know. We used to do silly things to relieve the tension: send rude messages to each other on our computers, put the customer on speaker-phone so that everyone could have a laugh — that kind of thing.

'Our supervisor was a complete fool. Nobody had any respect for her at all. We all wondered how she got the job in customer service in the first place: she had no idea about how to manage people. She had annoying habits and would invade your personal space: not saying anything but standing right up close to you and breathing down your neck.

'The low point for her came when we all went to the pub one night after work and one of us set fire to her hair! The worst thing was, she was so drunk that she didn't even notice. Somebody threw some beer on it, but all you could smell in the pub after that was singed hair. She kept saying: "Can anybody smell that smell?" but we all said: "No. What smell?" After that, nobody took her seriously in any way, though we still paid her the lip-service of respect for her position.

'Finally, she left, and they made me supervisor. I had one particular friend from the division and we used to see each other on the weekend. When I was promoted, she didn't really understand that I couldn't fool around like I did before. She started making nasty cracks about how I thought I was so much better than everybody else now that I was in a position of power, which wasn't true. I was just trying to do my job.

'The company was setting up another customer service division, and so they were downsizing the present one. I was told to start cutting down everybody's hours. I cut down everybody's hours so that they were all even — unfortunately my friend had more hours than everybody else.

'She came into the office, shut the door and yelled at me for ten minutes. She said I was a bitch, she said that that wasn't the way you treat friends and that if it was her in my position, she would have made sure that I wasn't cut at all. She said I had no loyalty at all. All I was doing was being fair to everybody. We don't speak anymore.'

INSTINCT

Listen to this little voice. It is the only infallible way of knowing if what you are doing is the right thing. It will tell you everything you need to know. If you feel a situation is not quite right, then it probably isn't. Faintly, in the back of your mind, you will hear a noise. These are alarm bells going off. They are trying to tell you something. What they are trying to tell you, more often than not, is that disaster is on the way. If you have a vague feeling of disquiet during the day, then rest assured that it will materialise at some point into a real issue of concern. Use your instinct when people ask you to do things, and in your opinion of others. If you feel that somehow, inexplicably, somebody is going to do you wrong, they probably are. If not now, then at some point in the future. Be wary, that's what your instinct is telling you.

THE LAST WORD

As we discussed in the beginning of this book, work appears to be a lot like a relationship with one crucial difference: one usually chooses the person with whom one has a relationship, but one cannot choose the people with whom one works. People often walk into a new job with the same expectations they have in a new relationship: happiness, trust, loyalty, honesty and perhaps a bit of fun. Woeful is the day when expectations are dashed and hopes are ruined.

Dazed, the unhappy lover wanders around saying: 'But why has this happened to me? What did I do to deserve this?' The answer, of course, is that nobody knows the answer to that question. The unhappy worker wanders around asking the same questions not knowing that the simple reason this particular relationship didn't work was because they didn't know the rules. When things start going wrong, the unhappy employee bores everybody within earshot with tales of the shortcomings of the office. ('I tell you, the woman never picks up her clothes. She is such a slob. I don't know why I bother with her.') When the relationship begins to become unstuck, the unhappy worker doesn't know which way to fall: should they get rid of them and find another partner, a new life, or try and patch things up? When the unhappy worker is pitched out of the organisation it's like a cuckolded lover wailing: 'But you said that we would be together forever, that you would love me forever. What went wrong?' And when the unhappy worker finally leaves, the recriminations can be as bitter, cynical and hostile as any divorce.

Any relationship is a gamble, personal ones more than most. Unlike the personal relationship, however, there are some rules at work that can help you to get along and to make the most of the job you have been employed to do. As I've outlined, these rules are invisible and difficult, but if you follow them you have a good chance of making your job enjoyable and fulfilling.

The important thing about any relationship is to have a few expectations, but not too many. Demand to be treated with respect, but don't expect it. Hope that people will behave in a reasonable and civilised manner, but don't ever expect that they will. Maintain, at all times, as detached and philosophical manner as you can manage. If you do manage to play the game successfully, then chances are that you yourself will be placed in a position of power. When this time comes, you will need to decide whether you will perpetuate the old regime, with all its problems, or think up a new way of running things that is based on respect, honesty and trust.

In 1516 the Tudor biographer, historian and thinker Sir Thomas More wrote a book called *Utopia*. In it, he explained a method of organising a society based on people's natural abilities. At the top of the tree was the Philosopher King. The Philosopher King was a detached person, ego-less and thus able to make the right kind of decisions at the right time. If you ever make it into management, maybe it's time for a new breed of manager, the Philosopher Manager, who is not plagued by insecurities, low self-esteem or ego, but is determined to let every person do the job they were employed to do, fulfil their potential and have a bit of fun along the way.

People who can help you

DEPARTMENT OF INDUSTRIAL RELATIONS
If you have a complaint and are not in a union, the Department of Industrial Relations (DIR) will investigate your complaint.

New South Wales	(02) 266 0688
Victoria	(03) 9 649 4545
Queensland	(07) 3 227 8060
South Australia	(08) 237 6966
West Australia	(09) 278 8800
Tasmania	(002) 35 1912
Northern Territory	(089) 81 7788
Australian Capital Territory	(06) 247 0144

LABOUR COUNCILS
The Labour Council in your state should be able to tell you which union and awards your job comes under.

Labour Council of NSW	(02) 264 1691
Victorian Trades Hall Council	(03) 9 639 2799
United Trades and Labour Council of South Australia	(08) 212 3155
United Trades and Labour Council of West Australia	(09) 444 6988
United Trades and Labour Council of Northern Territory	(089) 41 0001
United Trades and Labour Council of Tasmania	(002) 287 866
United Trades and Labour Council of ACT	(06) 247 7844
ACTU — Queensland Branch	(07) 3 846 2468

HUMAN RIGHTS AND EQUAL OPPORTUNITY COMMISSION

If you feel you have been discriminated against at work, contact either your union, or the Human Rights and Equal Opportunity Commission in your state.

New South Wales
Ph: (02) 284 9600
Toll Free: 1800 021 199
Fax: (02) 284 9611

Victoria
Ph: (03) 9 670 1951
Toll Free: 1800 134 142
Fax: (03) 9 670 2922

Queensland
Ph: (07) 3 844 6099
Toll Free: 1800 177 822
Fax: (07) 3 846 2211

Cairns
Ph: (070) 317 399
Toll Free: 1800 803 271
Fax: (070) 312 127

Rockhampton
Ph: (079) 226 877
Toll Free: 008 804 288
Fax: (079) 226 772

South Australia
Ph: (08) 226 5660
Toll Free: 008 188 163
Fax: (08) 223 3285

West Australia
Ph: (09) 222 8999
Toll Free: 008 198 149
Fax: (09) 222 9026

Tasmania
Ph: (002) 343 599
Fax: (002) 310 773

Northern Territory
Ph: (089) 819 111
Fax: (089) 411 508

Australian Capital Territory
Ph: (06) 247 3002
Fax: (06) 247 3358

Glossary of Terms

Alcohol	an instant hit with the stupid stick
Aliens	colleagues
Benevolent despotism	work
Best case scenario	all the things you've done
Best friend	Angie or Robert from down the road
Boomerang	an earlier disaster that comes back to haunt you
Boredom	social functions that are work-related
Brown noser	boss's best mate
Clayton's Deadline	early (your own) deadline
Closed-mouth smile	danger
Competence	credibility
Confidential exchange	a bartering chip
Daydreaming	subconscious desire working overtime
Democracy	a system of government that is not work-related
Difficult to work with	institutionalisation imminent
Disaster	sex at work
Disaster and indigestion	sex at lunchtime
Excess	when the company is paying
Free lunch	work functions
FYI	for your information
God	the Ultimate Boss
Instinct	alarm bells
King or Queen	managing director
Lamingtons	bribes
Landed gentry	middle management
Left field	the source of nasty, unforeseen questions

Life raft	fellow disaster survivor
Mistake	incorrect decision
Monkey	someone else's problem
Niceness	intelligence
Nobles	senior management
Open bar	work Christmas party or 'drink until you drop'
Pay	never enough
Perception	reality
Perks	bonus extras — anything you don't pay for
Personal problems	nervous breakdown
Peter Principle	everybody rises to the level of their own incompetence
Pulse	basic requirement for the job
Rarity	common sense
Reason	excuse
Resignation	liberation
Reward	money
Schmoozing	information gathering
Serfs	workers
Spreader	worker who requires large amount of horizontal room for papers
Stacker	worker who requires large amount of vertical room for papers
Toothy grin	friend
Village Idiot	inability to speak
Window of Opportunity	the time it takes to remedy a mistake
Workspeak	the language of the workplace
Worst case scenario	all the things you haven't done

Useful books to read

- *1984*, George Orwell, Penguin.
  What happens when the state controls everything. Newspeak and doublethink sections are particularly interesting.

- *Sophie's World*, Josteein Gardner, Orion Books.
  A crash course in philosophy.

- *Learned Optimism*, Martin Seligman, Random House.
  Shows that optimism is the primary quality for success.

- *Charming Up Profits*, Stephen Downes, Sally Milner Publishing.
  The guide to dress and manners at work.

- *Lunch*, Karen Moline, Picador.
  Terrible things can happen over lunch.

- *Bliss*, Peter Carey, UQP.
  What happens to people who don't have any philosophy or ethics. Particularly good for those who work in advertising.

- *Emotional Intelligence*, Daniel Goleman, Bloomsbury.
  This US psychologist redefines what it means to be smart: when it comes to success 'brainpower' as measured by IQ may actually matter less than 'character'.

- *More, Please*, Barry Humphries, Penguin.
  Shows that even successful characters are failures at some kinds of work.

- *What to Ask When You Don't Know What to Say: 555 Powerful Questions to Use for Getting Your Way at Work*, Sam Deep and Lyle Sussman, Prentice Hall.

- *Utopia*, Sir Thomas More, Everyman.

Useful films to see

🎬 *Dangerous Liaisons* (1988, US), Glenn Close, John Malkovich, Michelle Pfeiffer, Uma Thurman

An adaptation of Christopher Hampton's play *Les Liaisons Dangereuses* in which an unscrupulous woman manipulates the lives of those around her for amusement, with the help of a like-minded Count. It is the workplace transferred to eighteenth century France — some fine examples of Workspeak, creating diversions and plotting and scheming in general.

🎬 *Absolutely Fabulous* (1993–95, UK), Jennifer Saunders, Joanna Lumley, Julia Sawalha

Two ageing hippies, Patsy and Edwina, engage in a variety of politically-incorrect activities in this satirical, black comedy series, including drinking, drug-taking and sex to excess in a bid to convince themselves they are still young and have their whole lives ahead of them — how to get what you want, when you want it and still have a good time.

🎬 *The Last Seduction* (1995, US), Linda Fiorentino

A beautiful, ambitious, ruthless woman working in telemarketing uses her charm and feminine wiles to get ahead in this satirical look at callous 'get-to-the-top' behaviour — what happens when you let sex interfere with work.

🏛 *Reality Bites* (1993, US), Winona Ryder, Ethan Hawke

A group of college graduates go out into the real world. A good example of alienation in one's first job — Ryder's character, who works on a kitsch morning television program, does the revenge thing in a way that most of us can only dream about.

🏛 *2001 — A Space Odyssey* (1968, UK), Keir Dullea, William Sylvester, Gary Lockwood

Director Stanley Kubrick's film, adapted from Arthur C Clarke's book, where space travel is placed in the context of human history, from first confrontation with a 'greater power' to future time warp. It's humanity versus machinery of its own making in an unforgettable space journey with computer HAL in control — a timely warning on how technology can drop you in it.

🏛 *The Candidate* (1972, US), Robert Redford, Peter Boyle, Don Porter, Allen Garfield

This brilliant political satire offers fine examples of schmoozing and Polispeak, with Redford talked into running for Senate with the promise of absolute integrity in his campaign.

🏛 *Aliens* (1986, US), Sigourney Weaver, Paul Reiser, Carrie Henn

Weaver's character returns with a Marine squadron to the planet on which the ruthless alien creatures were originally discovered. Her mission? To wipe them out. A whole colony of these face-sucking, crawly parasites are uncovered, but how do you destroy a bunch of aliens who see you as food for their ultimate survival? Yep, sounds a lot like work!

The New Age (1994, US), Judy Davis, Peter Weller

Black comedy about the types of people who believe that everything requires the same kind of focus as work does; the sort of people who do courses on how to buckle their shoes. Brilliant scene of the protagonist yuppie trying to sell pens over the phone.

Citizen Kane (1941, US), Orson Welles, Joseph Cotton, Agnes Moorehead

Welles's first and best film that broke all the rules and invented some new ones in the fascinating story of a Hearst-like publisher's rise to power, which just goes to show — being rich and successful doesn't stop you from longing for the one thing you can't have.

Games That Mother Never Taught You (1982, US), Loretta Swit

A telemovie transferred to video, this shows the troubles encountered by a woman promoted to management. This film spells out 'corporate game' and shows what happens to people who don't know the rules.

Working Girl (1988, US), Sigourney Weaver, Melanie Griffith, Harrison Ford, Alec Baldwin

Comedy about a naive but ambitious secretary who tries to 'outwit' (read: shaft) her boss by pretending to be somebody she's not — good examples of dressing for success, and a happy ending to the usually tortuous scenario of sleeping with somebody you work with.

🎬 *Nine to Five* (1980, US), Jane Fonda, Lily Tomlin, Dolly Parton

Three savvy secretaries have to contend with an idiot boss, and inadvertently find their chance to take revenge with originality and wit — a dream come true.

🎬 *Norma Rae* (1979, US), Sally Field, Beau Bridges, Ron Leibman

Field's Oscar-winning performance as a real-life, poor, Southern textile worker gradually won over to unionisation by NYC labour organiser. Shows how standing up for your beliefs and not giving in to standover tactics can sometimes get you not only what you want, but what you deserve.

🎬 *Lost in America* (1985, US), Albert Brooks, Julie Haggerty

Two yuppies drop out of the rat-race and take to the road in this hilarious satire of upwardly-mobile yuppie types. Goes to show that if you want to chuck it in, you'd better be sure you know what you're doing and why, and don't have some ridiculous romantic notion of life outside the corporate world.